T0247764

"This is the best thing I've read about how to become a television writer. Not 'how to write a television script,' but 'how to become a television writer'! Anton has lucidly and comprehensively and entertainingly described the real-world process of getting in the door and getting a job writing for TV. If this is your dream, I can't think of a more valuable book to help you achieve it."

—David Kohan, Creator/Showrunner, *Will & Grace*

"In the past, when people asked me for advice on breaking into TV writing, I'd say 'Good luck, and please don't ask me to read your spec script!' Now I have a better answer: Read Anton Schettini's book. It's filled with specific, practical, up-to-date information— steps you can take that will work, because they worked for Anton (I know, because I hired him as a writer's assistant and watched him ascend through the ranks.) Buy it now—and don't ask him to read your spec script."

—Bob Daily, Executive Producer, *The Wonder Years*, *Superior Donuts*, *The Odd Couple*, *Desperate Housewives*; Co-Executive Producer, *Frasier*

"Many are called to write for television, but few are chosen. Of the thousands of aspiring writers I've encountered in over forty years of teaching, Anton Schettini is among that happy few who actually managed to become one. Now he's written a book that will help others who want to do the same. The advice he gives is specific, candid, and based on up-to-the-minute experience in the ever-mutating profession. It's not only the most pragmatic guide of its kind for those who want to write TV, but it's also an insightfully fun book for those who just like to watch it."

—Robert Thompson, Director, Bleier Center for Television and Popular Culture, Syracuse University

"This entertaining, informative, and engaging book is a must if you're looking to break into TV writing, but it's also an incisive and funny look at how TV gets made even if you're not. Buy it for your friends, and keep it from your enemies at all costs!"

—Nathaniel Stein, Writer, *Angie Tribeca*,
Curb Your Enthusiasm; Author, *The Threat*

"This book—written from the perspective of someone who not only survived the climb up the TV ladder, but thrived—should be required reading in every screenwriting program on every campus in America. Anton Schettini has produced a book that is informative, funny, and full of valuable inside info. Most important, it is bracingly clear-eyed—pulling precisely zero punches about the struggles that await anyone hoping to launch a career in this business. Breaking Into TV Writing is the essential read for anyone with dreams of writing for television. How I wish it had existed when I was starting out!"

—Michael Price, Creator/Showrunner, *F Is for Family*; Co-Executive Producer, *The Simpsons*

"So many hurdles! You might be the most talented of writers and have great scripts to peddle, but if you can't even get producers and executives to read your work, your career will go nowhere. Anton Schettini discovered that first-hand when starting out, but then he developed a strategy for overcoming those hurdles and became a success. Many books focus on writing craft and technique—this book explains steps you should take to actually become a working TV writer."

—Evan Smith, Author, *Writing Television Sitcoms*

BREAKING INTO TV WRITING

BREAKING INTO TV WRITING

How to Get Your First Job, Build Your Network, and Claw Your Way Inside the Writers' Room

ANTON SCHETTINI

TURNER
PUBLISHING COMPANY

Turner Publishing Company
Nashville, Tennessee

www.turnerpublishing.com

Cover design: Katarina Naskovski
Book Design: William Ruoto

Library of Congress Cataloging-in-Publication Data
Names: Schettini, Anton, author.
Title: Breaking into TV writing : how to get your first job, build your network, and claw your way inside the writers' room / Anton Schettini.
Description: Nashville, Tennessee : Turner Publishing Company, [2024] |
    Includes bibliographical references and index.
Identifiers: LCCN 2023010225 (print) | LCCN 2023010226 (ebook) | ISBN
    9781684429868 (hardcover) | ISBN 9781684429875 (paperback) | ISBN
    9781684429882 (epub)
Subjects: LCSH: Television authorship--Vocational guidance. | Television writers.
Classification: LCC PN1992.7 .S365 2024 (print) | LCC PN1992.7 (ebook) |
    DDC 808.2/25--dc23
LC record available at https://lccn.loc.gov/2023010225
LC ebook record available at https://lccn.loc.gov/2023010226

Printed in the United States of America

1 2 3 4 5 6 7 8 9 10

To my niece and nephew, Ruby and Dominic, who inspire the hell out of me every day.

To Ione, whose never-ending encouragement kept me going when publishing my own book seemed like a pipe dream.

CONTENTS

FOREWORD

BY LAWRENCE KONNER

WARNING!

If either one of your parents is the head of a studio or network, save your money and don't bother buying this book. For the rest of you, read on.

I've been writing TV for decades. My credits include *The Sopranos* and *Boardwalk Empire*. I've written features such as *Mona Lisa Smile* and *The Many Saints of Newark*. And now I'm stuck writing the foreword to some book about beginning your TV writing career. How in the hell did this happen?

Well, it's because the author, Anton Schettini, asked. And more importantly, he made the connections necessary to get in touch with me in the first place. This is precisely the type of networking you'll need to do and the types of connections you'll need to make if you want to pursue a career in TV. It's one thing to write a great script. It's a completely different thing to know how to get that script to the right person. Anton's recent experience breaking into TV writing is invaluable for anybody taking a crack at making a career out of being a TV writer. The assistant jobs, writing jobs, samples you need, and writers' rooms you are looking to get into are entire worlds unto themselves. This book will teach you how to navigate those worlds.

When I began my TV writing career, the broadcast model was firmly in place. If your writing was good enough, you could get your script into the hands of an agent or a showrunner. They could get you into a writers' room. You could rely on a "staffing season," a specific time during the year when TV shows hired writers. Your job, if done well, could last for an entire year or for multiple seasons.

It wasn't easy, but there was, at the very least, a system that remained in place up until the last twenty years or so, with streaming services supplanting networks and cable channels. For better and for worse, streaming has changed the business. But what's remained consistent is the fact that your network matters. If you have no one to send your script to, your screenplay will remain the unseen material of a mere hobbyist.

TV writing is a difficult pursuit and an even more difficult profession. There will be dark moments when you question why you're doing it at all. That's why, when entering your career, you need to know that you enjoy the writing. You need to enjoy reading scripts and writing scripts and figuring out your style of writing. You need to enjoy rewriting and perfecting your style so your voice comes through and cuts across the heaps of scripts landing on executives' and producers' desks every day.

Anton lays a foundation to help you understand the nature of the business and prepare yourself mentally for a career in the arts, or at least the arts-adjacent world of commercial screenwriting. The TV business is in flux, and there's not one assured trajectory. This book will lay the groundwork for what you need to know to begin carving out your own path in a quickly changing industry.

FLIP THE DOLPHIN

There's a story in writers' room lore that goes like this: A room of comedy writers wanted to prank one of the new writers on the staff. But they didn't want an easy prank; they wanted to challenge themselves. One day, when their target was out of the room, they settled on an intricate plan. They would come up with a nonsensical phrase and give it a meaning. Everyone would start using that phrase in the "proper" context with the goal of making the prankee so accustomed to the phrase that they would absorb the meaning and use it themselves. The ultimate goal was not just for the mark to use the phrase, but to use it properly and without any coaching from anyone.

The phrase the writers settled on was "flip the dolphin." The meaning of the phrase was decided to be "changing the order of two words or sentences." For example, if anybody in the room thought Larry's line should come before Maria's, they might say "let's flip the dolphin on Larry and Maria's lines."

The writers got to work. Well, not real work. Prank work. For weeks, the writers chose the best times to use—but not overuse— the phrase in the right context. The mark never asked what the phrase meant and was seemingly completely unbothered by it altogether. It looked like a lost cause. Then one day, the prankee spoke up with a pitch. "Hey, can we take those two words and flip the dolphin?" The room erupted to the shock of the stunned writer who had unknowingly been successfully trained in utter nonsense.

The made-up phrase lives on, still used across the industry as a real phrase with no irony, and oftentimes used by writers who have no knowledge of its origins.

This story is important for a few reasons, not the least of which being proof that writers' rooms are ridiculous places. More importantly, I wrote this book to "flip the dolphin" (See what I did there?), on what is generally taught about how to break into TV writing. So often, I hear seasoned writers declare "If you're a good writer, you'll succeed," and "Just work on your writing and everything else will fall into place." But writing is only a small part of being successful in the industry. There's an entire ecosystem and landscape within the TV writing world that you need to learn to navigate to reach a point where your writing ability matters. It's only when you discover the ins and outs of the industry, and commit to moving up within it, that you can push beyond being a writer for an audience of one and start treating screenwriting like a career.

When you first begin exploring a career in TV, or learning about the industry in college, you'll be presented with a lot of rules to follow, paths to take, and dues to pay. However, much like the phrase "flip the dolphin," many of these supposed rules were created by somebody somewhere down the line because it suited them at the time. In the same way that it's crucial to know the rules of screenwriting craft so that you can bend, twist, and break them to your advantage, understanding the known points of entry and how people before you got their start gives you the right foundation to start breaking norms and carving your own path.

Maybe you're awed by the writing on certain television shows. Or maybe you spend every day shouting from the rooftops how much better a writer you are than the people who write most of the crap on television. Either way, the actual writing is only half of it. There are very talented people who make it nowhere, and there are talentless people who make it very far. There's a huge difference between someone with a good script and someone who is pursuing their goal out in the real world, meeting the people they need to meet and pushing themselves in the right direction to create an actual career in TV.

I'm already hearing the hesitation. *Meet the people I need to meet? Push myself in the right direction? Sounds like a half-assed Tony Robbins speech.* I know, and you're right. Those are the same vague points of advice I heard over and over again when I was starting my TV writing career. That doesn't mean they're wrong, but it doesn't give you any practical steps to follow to move forward. This book was written to give you those practical steps and to demystify a mystifying industry with seemingly no clear path. And, while it's true that there's no defined corporate ladder-style trajectory to becoming a TV writer, there are jobs that can help you get there, there are people you can meet who can get you closer, and there's an entire industry to learn how to navigate to reach your goal of writing for TV.

I'm not trying to make you a better writer. There are far more experienced, smarter, better-looking, better-smelling writers than me who can teach you screenwriting craft. And while screenwriting skills are important, it is only a part of becoming a TV writer. This book will lay a foundation for what the TV writing world is like, how it's changed, how it's changing, and, based on personal experience and the experiences of my friends and colleagues, how to best position yourself to become a part of it and thrive within it.

Becoming familiar with the TV writing landscape will do a few things for you:

- Help you decide if this career is for you.

- Prove to you that anybody can do it.
- Give you a game plan for beginning your career.

By the end of this book, you will know:

- How an episode of TV is made.
- How a TV writers' room works.
- The various jobs inside a writers' room.
- Which jobs can help your career.
- How to use your job to your greatest advantage.
- Which jobs should be avoided at all costs (including asshole-boss red flags).
- How to search for jobs (including websites to start your job search).
- How streaming has upended the TV industry and how that presents both a problem and an opportunity.
- How the 2023 WGA writers' strike has affected up-and-coming writers.
- What script samples you need.
- How to get people to read your script.
- How to evolve with a constantly evolving industry.
- How to craft a compelling list that leaves you wanting more.

CHAPTER 1

WHY SHOULD WE LISTEN TO YOU?

I have been working in television for over a decade in a variety of roles such as production assistant, executive assistant, writers' production assistant, night production assistant, writers' assistant (Are you seeing a theme here?), script coordinator, and, finally, writer—the holy grail of television jobs. In TV, the writers are the be-all and end-all. They decide what happens in every episode of every season, and they are even the final word on a set. A scene isn't done shooting until the writer tells the director they are clear to move on. Unlike feature films, where the director takes over as soon as the studio buys the writer's script, in TV the director is a hired gun. With the exception of a few new IP-based entities like Marvel, in which executives, and sometimes director/producers, oversee much of the writing, the TV writer, specifically the showrunner, is who everyone looks to for answers.

I grew up on shows like *Seinfeld*, *The Simpsons*, and *24*, and witnessed the rise of prestige TV with *The Wire*, *The Sopranos*, and *Breaking Bad*. I figured all this creativity and fun must start in the writers' room. So I made it my mission to get in there and see what this room was all about. And I got there, fairly quickly . . . in a supporting role. And I stayed there, for a fairly long time . . . in a supporting role.

What started as a quick jump into a giant comedy on the Warner

Bros. lot turned into a steady slog in assistant roles throughout the Los Angeles studio lot ecosystem. I have worked at the Warner Bros. lot, the Sony lot, both CBS lots, the Fox lot, the NBC Universal lot, and a slew of *Being John Malkovich*-esque offices around Hollywood full of egos bigger than the office space itself. I've worked on eleven broadcast network shows, two streaming shows, and six pilots. In fact, I've worked on more major studio television productions than many seasoned writers I've encountered in the industry.

Here are some of the shows I've worked on that you may have heard of:

- *2 Broke Girls* (CBS)
- *Will & Grace* (NBC)
- *The Goldbergs* (ABC)
- *F Is for Family* (Netflix)
- *The Late Show with David Letterman* (CBS)

Here are some of the shows I've worked on that you probably *haven't* heard of:

- *One Big Happy* (NBC)
- *Partners* (CBS)
- *Schooled* (ABC)
- *Indebted* (NBC)
- *Happy Together* (CBS)
- *Superior Donuts* (CBS)
- *Ground Floor* (TBS)
- *Snap* (AMC Networks)

Here are some of the shows I've worked on that you *definitely* haven't heard of (because they never made it past the pilot stage):

- *Relatively Happy* (NBC)
- *The 46 Percenters* (ABC)
- *My Three Husbands* (NBC)
- *Gotham* (not the one you've heard of; this one was about sexy magicians or something) (Fox)

I pursued a career on the comedy side of the TV landscape before moving over to drama and now oscillating between the two. My early career was made up of the most traditional style of TV, the multi-camera comedy. These are the TV shows filmed in a studio set with an audience. (Yes, what you thought was canned laughter is actually real laughter that is "sweetened." More on that later.) This was most of what you saw on TV back in the day—*Taxi, Mary Tyler Moore, Friends.* Now, it's anything bright, colorful, and probably watched by your grandmother.

Multi-Cam Comedies: Four cameras shoot a scene simultaneously in a set. There is a studio audience and the whole production feels like a play.

Single-Cam Comedies: Filmed like a movie, one shot at a time; this is what most comedy is today—*Ted Lasso, Abbott Elementary, Barry.* (Hint: when you don't hear laughter, it's single-cam.)

Multi-cam comedies were my bread and butter as I was coming up. And unfortunately, in the years I was working on them, the Nielsen ratings dropped lower and lower, and networks didn't know what to do about it.

Nielsen Ratings: A system by which special cable boxes that track viewership are given out all over the country. An approximate number of viewers is then extracted to give an average rating for each show on TV. They now have a different system for tracking streaming.

So they canceled shows quickly, which doesn't allow you to grow within a company and move up. Therefore, my early career in TV, as is the case with many people in entertainment, was patched together with short-term gigs within and outside of the industry.

Here are some of the jobs I've had to support myself between productions:

- ESL teacher
- HR assistant at UCLA
- Mattress salesman
- Gelato scooper
- Busboy
- Waiter
- Copywriter for an Ohio-based bee removal service
- Copywriter for the National Lottery of Malta
- Copywriter for a genital-cooling seat cushion
- Toy demonstrator at FAO Schwarz
- Caterer
- Soup ladler at The Soup Man (*Seinfeld*'s The Soup Nazi)
- Stockperson at a German dildo warehouse (okay, that was a fellow TV assistant's job that I was jealous of because they got free pizza on Friday)
- "Guide to getting your start in TV" author

These days, with these quickening cancellations, instead of getting to know people and earning your stripes at one show, you're out on the street with no insurance and, if you're lucky, starting over again at a new show. If you're unlucky, you're getting free pizza while moving boxes of German dildos.

Meanwhile, on the cable and streaming side, TV shows are getting shorter episode orders and they're running for fewer seasons. As a viewer, this was a positive development. I never needed to see Ross get a kid, I didn't need to see the *Lost* writers pretend they knew where the story was going all along, and I certainly didn't need to see Fonzi "jump the shark." TV show creators are now allowed to pursue their vision for a series, as opposed to being forced to wring every dollar out of a hit. But as somebody trying to make a living out of TV, it means your gigs don't last as long and there are fewer opportunities to move up.

Jump the Shark: In season 5, episode 3 of *Happy Days*, Fonzi water-skis over a shark. It was a hijinks-laden episode that deviated completely from where the series had begun. The term "jump the shark" is now used to describe when a TV show has gone too far and is no longer what it used to be.

This is one of the many idiosyncrasies of the evolving TV industry that I want to make you aware of before you embark on this crazy career. Knowing what you're getting into is essential before you dedicate your time, money, and sanity to this pursuit.

But we haven't heard of you, and you were an assistant forever. Why should we listen to you? Precisely because you haven't heard of me.

I'm a zero-award-winning, many-coffee-bringing, heavily seasoned assistant with very little clout and a few solid writing credits to my name.

When I was in college considering a career in TV, I looked high and low for anything written about screenwriting, and I found a ton of amazingly informative books that changed the way I wrote. But I couldn't find anything about the TV business itself and what it's like to work on a television show. The few TV writing books I did find were from somebody who had made it big years ago. They had broken in during the '90s and had been operating in a different industry altogether. Oftentimes, the way they got their break into the industry was not explained. These books didn't provide much useful actionable information because, unless you're Steven Spielberg Jr., you don't jump straight into being a writer. Heck, generally you can't even jump straight into being a writers' assistant. There are hoops for days—and I know them well because I called those hoops home for years. And those assistant hoops were good to me. They kept me working on big network shows, they kept a roof over my head, on two occasions they gave me a big ol' payday with a network script, and, more recently, my entertainment industry obstacle course has led to what I've been working my way toward all along.

In the past few years, I became the executive producer of a show on a streaming service, I've been able to pitch my own TV show ideas to most of the major studios and production companies, and my writing partner and I have a TV show in development at one of the biggest studios in town. But all that good stuff is still fairly new. In fact, up until the pandemic, I was still going from assistant job to assistant job, wondering when my break would come.

Writing Partner: Self-explanatory enough, this is somebody you write with and share credit with. But a lesser-known fact is you split a paycheck with them as well. There are pros and cons to this—con, less money; pro, showrunners looking to hire a writer are getting two for close to the price of one, which can be a very attractive proposition. Overall, if you enjoy writing with someone, have similar sensibilities or sensibilities that complement one another, it can be hugely helpful. My writing partner, Mark, and I met as assistants on a TV show called *Partners* (aww . . .). We've kept each other on track, motivated, and afloat during the hard times. Writing can be a very solitary pursuit. Having a writing partner helps alleviate that and makes you responsible to someone other than yourself, which, for many of us, chips away at our tendency to procrastinate.

The fact that my assistanting (a word I completely made up) is so recent makes me uniquely positioned to tell you exactly what the ground floor of TV is like as it's happening right now, across network and streaming in this post-pandemic, post-2023 WGA strike world. More importantly, I have current knowledge about what it takes to push beyond assistanting and start being paid as a writer.

In order to get to the somewhat more credentialed place I am now, I had to navigate the odd vague duties of a production assistant, the stressful minutiae of an executive assistant, the painstaking attention to detail of a writers' assistant, and, finally, the incredible stress and therapy-seeking that comes with being a script coordinator. I'm fine now. Everything's fine!

On top of that, I had to learn to recognize when I had wrung everything I could out of being an assistant and force myself to stop taking the assistant jobs I had previously worked so hard to get, change my trajectory, and try a different strategy.

In this book you'll find everything I wish I had been taught in school and everything I wish I had known before I moved to LA. That includes information about the practical everyday work you do in a television writers' room, from the production assistant up to the showrunner, and the process that churns out your favorite shows. There will be sarcasm, irony, and bitterness. There will be aggravating stories that will make you ask yourself "Do I really want this?" But then there will be happy stories that will make you go "Okay, maybe I *do* want this."

But isn't it all about the writing? Won't the best script make its way through and open doors for me? No. Great writing will help, but a great script isn't anything if the right person isn't reading it. It's the classic "if a screenplay falls in the woods and there's nobody there to hear it" dilemma. But, of course, one can't be a writer if one doesn't write. So, having the right material to send around when you make the right connections is crucial. Later in the book I'll discuss what types of scripts to have ready to show when you start to get your writing out there.

So, whether you call this a guide, a career book, or a well-structured rant, the following is my advice and knowledge from over a decade in the TV industry. My hope is that after reading this book, you will have a better understanding of the industry you're getting into, what practical steps you can take to get yourself into the position you want to be in, and how to avoid some of the major pitfalls that I succumbed to along the way.

A Note About Fridges: There is a weird phenomenon in LA in which rental apartments don't automatically come with a fridge. This has created a lively online market for used fridges. I have spent countless hours showing up at the doors of strangers, hand cart in tow, praying I don't break anything while a friend and I haul a monstrously large fridge out of their apartment, into a truck, and into our apartment.

When I first moved to LA, there were still areas where you could find some good deals on a place to live. That doesn't seem to be the case any longer. After a quick dip during the pandemic, rents have shot up everywhere. Because of the ridiculous prices, most people have roommates their first few years in LA, and often much longer than that.

As a person who's new to LA, be aware of what neighborhood you're moving into. If you're planning on working in an area that *looks* like it's a half hour away from your new apartment, just know that a half hour on a map is not a half hour in traffic. Areas that are "right next to" LA, like Long Beach, Pomona, or Anaheim, can mean a two-hour commute during rush hour just to go thirty miles. It's untenable. So, do yourself a favor and research the location and commute times before you decide on a place.

Unfortunately, you likely won't know where you'll be working. And worse yet, even if you do, jobs don't necessarily last very long. You may begin the year working on a show at Sony, only to finish the year working at Warner Bros., on the opposite side of the city. That said, it's helpful to know that most of the major studios are concentrated in Culver City, Burbank, Studio City, Downtown LA, and Hollywood, and, with a few exceptions, you can generally expect to work in one of those areas.

MY FAVORITE LOTS

One of the most nerve-racking experiences of my life was arriving for my interview at the Warner Bros. Studio lot for my first production assistant job. Upon entering this massive complex, you see the famous water tower in the distance and park in a structure that has spots reserved for the biggest directors in the industry. Entering the lot truly makes you feel like you've made it to—capital letters—HOLLYWOOD. So, to give you an idea of what your future "office" may look like, here's a description of some of my favorite lots I've worked in, along with some of their highlights and quirks.

Warner Bros. Studios

This is one of the largest lots in Los Angeles, equipped with some of the most fascinating exterior sets. There's a jungle moat that can be filled or drained (depending upon the needs of the scene) that was used for the backwoods of Louisiana in *True Blood*. There's a quaint midwestern square that became Stars Hollow in *Gilmore Girls*. And of course, there are multiple New York streets and alleyways that have been used in absolutely everything. There's even a stage so large that they were able to flood it with water and simulate fierce, intense waves for *The Perfect Storm*.

NBC Universal

The NBC lot is situated next to the Universal Studios Hollywood theme park, and, before I worked there, a passageway connected the two. People working on the lot could spend their lunch hour jumping on rides in the theme park and then go right back to their office. However, that passageway is now closed, leaving only the most enormous, impressive backlot to visit during breaks. It's full of Old West sets, the house from *Psycho*, and the main square from *Back to the Future*. In fact, the Studio Tour, which is an attraction in the theme park, takes you around to these various locations as well as a

Curriculum aside, universities are great for meeting lots of new people. Turns out college is really a giant networking event. You can learn most everything else on the job, but the connections you make are vital.

After graduating and moving back home, I started working some odd jobs to save money for an eventual move out of my parents' place. My friend from Syracuse told me *The Late Show with David Letterman* was hiring Pages. I interviewed and got the job. Even if you weren't a fan, everyone in the industry knew the importance that David Letterman and the Ed Sullivan Theater held over the TV landscape, and it was incredible to be a part of it.

The Page job was my first foray into the industry, and it was an odd one. In most people's minds, the job conjures images of Kenneth from *30 Rock*, answering phones and catering to the needs of the stars. My experience was not like that. At *The Late Show*, the Pages were a part of the audience department. This meant I was in charge of ticketing people for the show, corralling them into the theater, and then yelling the rules of the show to them like they were joke-heavy Miranda rights. This couldn't have been farther from the inner workings of a TV show. In fact, a lot of my time was spent just *outside* the theater, waiting for the show to start and getting asked questions by soon-to-be-audience members like "Do you get to meet Dave?" or "Do you know anything about that intern thing?" Not the most tactful bunch.

When the audience walked in to receive their free tickets, they were asked questions about the show. The questions were posed as a bit of fun trivia, but in reality their fandom was being assessed. If they were found to be true fans, they had to pass another obstacle: were they a young couple? If they got both these requirements out of the way, they were given a sticker on their ticket and were seated in one of the first two rows. If they didn't know the show at all, they were seated in the balcony.

This seating process was my first taste of what entertainment was going to be like—judgey. And although later in the book I will detail the various assistant jobs that can help you along your path to being a TV writer, I am discussing this one here because it is not one that will get you a TV writing job. It's possible that more Kenneth-style Page jobs at 30 Rockefeller Plaza will get you closer to the action. But that was not my experience at *The Late Show*.

My Page position lasted for nine months. When I was done, I left for South America and taught ESL, traveled around, and found myself—or whatever. That's for another book. After returning to the US, I packed my stuff and drove across the country to LA in my 1995 Honda Odyssey. The car had some quirky features. There was the classic tape player with an auxiliary cord that could be plugged into a portable CD player; air conditioning that, when turned on, would ever so slightly accelerate the car even when I didn't have my foot on the gas pedal; a leaky oil tank that required refilling every two hundred miles; and an exhaust pipe that, whenever I hit a bump, would disconnect from the muffler, making this soccer mom car sound like I was revving a V8.

THE EARLY YEARS IN LA

I pushed (sometimes literally) my scrappy heap of a car all the way to LA and moved in with friends who happened to be looking for a new apartment. These were friends from college and another example of how connections at school can help you later on. It was 2012, and my portion of the rent was $700 for a tiny room in a three-bedroom apartment. (Sorry to the new folks moving to Los Angeles; these rents probably don't exist anymore.)

Once I arrived in LA, I immediately started looking for jobs, and I got one relatively quickly off Craigslist. It was a production assistant/runner position working for a small production company that was responsible for producing pre-taped segments for a major the entertainment world. I worked as a writers' assistant for a couple of pilots, which I got through a prior relationship with a production coordinator at my first job at Warner Bros. I also worked as a writers' assistant for a show on Netflix, which I got through a fellow PA at a previous job. The connections from varying jobs and TV shows kept proving fruitful, even though the jobs were a combined six months of work. So I made ends meet with my temp jobs.

I stuck with it and kept in touch with as many of my connections and previous coworkers as possible, which turned out to be the most important thing I could have done. If you're not doing this, and you don't have a job that ties you in with the industry, then you can become disconnected very quickly, and all the hard work you've put in and good will you've accumulated can be washed away within a year.

Eventually, I got a job with a showrunner who was on an overall deal at Warner Bros. And even though they had a deal, they were not working on a show. In fact, their deal was ending soon, so they weren't expected to do much of anything. As this person's executive assistant, that lack of job duties was very cordially extended to me. My days were spent working in a windowless office on the Warner Bros. lot. Sometimes the showrunner would come in, sometimes they wouldn't. I got paid all the same.

BACK IN THE ROOM

When this showrunner eventually had a TV show again, I was made the writers' assistant. By this time, I had gotten to know a lot of people. I knew the script coordinator on this show, both showrunners, and many of the people working in the production office. As a result of building and maintaining these many connections, I was a shoo-in for the job.

I was only present during the initial writing stages of this new job, because there was a lot of crazy energy and yelling. Ooh, boy, the yelling. I wanted out of there as quickly as possible. I once watched the showrunner and another high-level writer chase each other around and through various offices Scooby Doo-style, trying to find and yell at each other. The showrunner would pop out of a door and yell "You do this every time!" The writer would pop out of a different door: "How dare you!" It would have been hilarious if it weren't riddled with HR violations.

FIRST TV WRITING CREDITS

Years earlier, during my first Warner Bros. PA job, I met my eventual writing partner, Mark. We were both trying to make our way through these assistant jobs and write scripts on the side. We had similar tastes in TV and writing styles and a similar growing exasperation with the industry, and things just clicked. So, when Mark told me there was an open position on his show, I jumped at the chance. Not only were the writers cool, but he had been given a freelance script there the year before.

Freelance Script: An episode of a TV show written by someone outside of the regular writing staff. Freelance scripts are often given to writers' assistants and script coordinators.

A freelance script is a huge deal to an assistant, and I was hopeful that the show would last long enough for me to get a taste. And it did! My years of assistanting hadn't led to nothing. Sure, the show would be canceled after one season of working on it, and there would be no chance to move up to a writer's role. But I had gotten that first TV credit.

After this abrupt and surprising cancellation, my showrunner recommended me to his showrunner friend. Another connection was made, and I worked on a new pilot, which eventually got picked up to series, and I was made the script coordinator on the show. Here, I was given another credit on an episode of network TV. And with a second television credit, and a really nice chunk of change, I became a member of the WGA, the Writers Guild of America.

Things were looking up. I had been in LA for six years and had two network scripts under my belt. I was pitching lots of jokes and getting attention in the writers' room. I was even promised a writing job if the show returned for the next year. Finally, there was a chance to move from assistant to official staff writer. However, those hopes would soon be dashed when the show was canceled after its thirteen-episode run. Still, I was a WGA writer and I had network credits to my name. Surely somebody was looking for what I had to offer . . . Turns out, nope. Despite the strides I had made proving myself to the other writers in the rooms I worked in, I was still not looked at as someone with experience as a writer. I was merely an experienced script coordinator who had gotten lucky with a couple of scripts.

WHEN ASSISTANTING GOES WRONG

Unemployed and watching my meager savings dwindle, I reached out to my network. I discovered that a line producer I had worked with on a pilot a year before happened to be hiring. So, after a few months of unemployment, I became a writers' assistant on a hit show run by a toxic person and filled with (nice but) sad writers. The showrunner would change things on a whim, forcing everybody in production and the writers' office to stay ungodly hours, giving up any sense of a life.

A few things I experienced as a writers' assistant on this show:

- People crying, like, all the time.
- At midnight, after a long and pointless rewrite, the

showrunner summoned his assistant from their bed so he could be picked up and brought home. He didn't want to walk the ten minutes across the lot to grab an Uber.
- To deter depression, a group of puppies was rented every year, placed in a pen, and everyone could pet them and let their sad out onto them.
- Four different bosses in the span of eight months.
- Being called in for a meeting to discuss the fact that I was "typing too loud."

THE CORONA RESET

To cap it all off, the final day of production was March 13, 2020. Anybody remember that day? It was a doozy, and a very fitting end to a terrible season. Like a lot of people, the pandemic led to a whole reexamination of my priorities. I vowed to not take another assistant job again. It wasn't that the jobs hadn't helped me along the way. But I had gotten everything I could out of them. They were no longer serving the purpose I needed them for, which was to progress, build a network, and become a writer. In spite of the fact that I was moving my way up the rungs of the assistant ladder, I began to realize that it didn't matter since everybody still thought of me as an assistant.

This caused a financial dilemma. If I was going to keep pursuing this career without the jobs that kept me financially stable . . . well, not stable . . . alive, I would need another way of making money. So, I started copywriting and freelancing. I got pretty good at it, too. In the meantime, I used the WGA's resources to reach out to every single production company and management company out there to try to resurrect some sort of a career pulse. My writing partner and I gave each other a task of ten emails a week. And it started to work. We were getting answers, we were having Zoom meetings, and eventually we signed with new managers.

Now, people have very different experiences with their representation. And finding an agent or a manager does not equate directly with "making it." But in our case, we found managers who were hungry, who would get us meetings with executives, and who scheduled pitches for many of the TV projects we'd been writing and developing. We were finally meeting people and making connections as writers, not as assistants.

FROM ASSISTANT TO WRITER

Eventually, we met another client of our managers' who was developing a show and pitching it to a subsidiary of AMC. It sold rather quickly and, since we had helped him practice and prepare the pitch, he asked us to be writers on the show. And just like that, we were executive producers on a drama for AMC Networks. And one of the many, many general meetings we'd had the year prior led to my writing partner and me going into development with a major studio.

This is a completely new and exciting phase of my career, and it's happening right now as I write this book. That is to say, I JUST broke through. For me, it took assistanting, networking, then *not* assistanting, and relentless emailing and phone calls. But no matter what job I was or wasn't doing, one thing remained consistent throughout: maintaining the relationships and connections I made at every stage meant everything.

I took a few PA gigs in LA that I found off Craigslist, which were outside of the major studios and networks. But after getting into the studio and network system, I never applied for another job again. I got every job because I knew somebody from somewhere I had worked before. This was possible because I was keeping in touch with people and was keeping myself at the top of their minds. I was also a good worker and was somebody that people wanted to work with. Keeping in touch with people doesn't mean much if they've worked with you before and had a bad experience. But they will genuinely want to help you if they had a good time working with you.

Just as important was that when I saw a dead end, I pivoted. Sure, it took me way too long, but I did it eventually. And when the opportunity arose, I had the scripts, writing knowledge, and writers' room experience to be competent and show that I was supposed to be there.

PART II

THE WRITERS' ROOM

Common discussions in a writers' room:

- Where to go for lunch
- Why that lunch place sucks
- Problems with the home or pool remodel
- Why that TV show that's a lot like the one you're working on but is much more popular sucks
- Why (insert current politician here) sucks
- Episode plot lines
- Who picked this lunch place? It sucks.
- Getting out of TV and becoming a therapist
- Getting out of TV and working at Trader Joe's ("they seem happy")
- LA traffic
- If it's okay to send the PA really far for this really good lunch spot
- Where to go for dinner

A writers' room is like a mad science experiment. What if we took anywhere from eight to seventeen highly artistic, unpredictable, creative, intelligent, and sometimes unhinged people and put them in a room for eight to fourteen hours a day? Now, fill them with greasy takeout food and repeat this daily for two to nine months. Oh, and let's add in a task with a deadline. Will people be driven mad? Yes. Will people be depressed? Most definitely. Will there be a lot of stimulating and/or hilarious conversation? For sure.

"The room," as it's called, is like an all-day conference meeting. The writers sit around a table starting at 10 a.m. and talk about story. In the meantime, the writers' assistant or script coordinator takes copious notes on what is being discussed. Much of the time, however, is spent discussing anything other than the story at hand. This can include food, politics, or funny stories from other writers' rooms.

In the room, tempers flare, glances are noticed, people fall asleep, some writers devolve into disgusting or hilarious versions of themselves. Many writers' rooms won't let out until the wee hours of the morning. Successful shows like *Friends*, which notoriously wouldn't start actually writing until the evening, perpetuated this as the ideal for being a successful show. This tendency has persisted in the comedy world until today. So, I say on behalf of every assistant and writer who has worked at the office until daybreak, damn you, *Friends*, and your ultra-charming relatable-ness.

My experience has mostly been in network comedy rooms, a beast unto themselves. However, the larger themes, script phases, and jobs can be explained across the board from single- and multi-cam comedy to drama. So, let's start with who is in a room from the bottom up.

CHAPTER 4

THE WRITERS

The writer hierarchy starts at staff writer and goes up to executive producer/showrunner, and though there are differences in pay and what's expected of the various roles in between, most of the titles don't mean anything in terms of the jobs themselves. Many people watching TV at home see "Executive Story Editor" and think "That's so specific, it must have clearly delineated duties in the writers' room." Not the case. It's just a title that gives the writer a specific minimum, based on the WGA union contract, and denotes your seniority level. Still, if you want to be in the TV world, it's important to know the ladder you'll be climbing. Because even though the titles are essentially meaningless, they do equate to wildly different amounts of power, money, and cachet. The following is a clear layout of the different writers in a writers' room, from the bottom all the way up to the top.

(*Note: When indicated, the salary figures presented are WGA minimums [scale] for nondevelopment writers' rooms as regulated by the initial figures in the 2023 WGA contract. These numbers will rise slightly over the three years of the contract. Other salaries were pulled from the WGA's Writers' Deal Hub Series Compensation Guide, which was last published in December 2021. Because these figures are always in flux, use the following to get an approximate idea of the salary range for each position.*)

STAFF WRITER

You've made it into the hallowed grounds of TV writing. This is a starting position for any writer on a TV show. As a staff writer, you are not expected to chime in as much as the upper- and mid-level writers. It's important for the staff writer to choose their pitches and thoughts carefully and lay them out succinctly. Since you're still proving yourself, you don't get the benefit of the doubt. In a comedy room, a successful staff writer is often one who is quick with a great joke that keeps the room from getting stuck. A good story pitch gets tossed and turned around in the room, and it's hard for the showrunner to decipher who it came from or where it started. But a good joke gets credit immediately. And when you're in this position, credit is important.

Traditionally, staff writer positions were thought of as learning positions. This was a way to get new writers used to the writers' room and learn on the job. However, those days are over, and today, staff writers are expected to understand how to write a TV show.

It can be difficult to negotiate more than scale, the union-designated minimum salary for a staff writer, because you're new to the scene and usually this is your first time being employed as a writer. That being said, scale for a staff writer is still a great weekly rate.

Staff Writer salary based on WGA minimums (Scale): $4,362 to $5,567 per week, depending on the number of guaranteed weeks.

STORY EDITOR/EXECUTIVE STORY EDITOR

Story editors are often writers who are working on their second season on a TV show. Generally, each year you're hired back from the prior season, you get a title bump. However, with multiple-season shows becoming increasingly less common, it becomes harder to move up. In fact, many staff writers are now forced to repeat their entry-level position multiple times before moving up to story editor.

Therefore, the story editor can be a relatively young or first-time writer who has been on one show for two years, or it can be somebody who's been around a long time and has had the misfortune of being on canceled show after canceled show.

Executive story editors represent the highest level among the lower-level writers and, like story editors, they get bumped up to this role based on negotiation or number of years at a show.

Story editors and executive story editors don't have the negotiating power that the upper- and mid-level writers do, and, like staff writers, will also often have to take scale. (As I mentioned before, scale is amazing!)

Story Editor and Executive Story Editor salaries based on WGA minimums (Scale): $7,783 to $10,382 per week, depending on the number of guaranteed weeks.

CO-PRODUCER/PRODUCER/SUPERVISING PRODUCER

These are the mid-level writers, and the titles are once again arbitrary, but they do represent the middle of the pack in terms of seniority and years in TV writing. A writer in this category is expected to know the writing process and be able to fill any niche that's needed by the showrunner. These positions often come with producing responsibilities, which include rewriting lines on set if something in the script isn't working, communicating with actors, and, if the showrunner's not on set, being the liaison between the showrunner and the director.

Salaries based on the WGA Series Compensation Guide:
Median salary: $15.75k to $20.5k per episode
Maximum salary: $43.75k per episode

CO-EXECUTIVE PRODUCER

There are usually two or three Co-Execs on every show. They are seasoned writers who have a long track record of TV writing jobs. A showrunner will usually give more credence to what a Co-Exec is pitching than to any other writer. However, I've seen rooms where the staff writer (the lowest writer) or even the script coordinator (an assistant) gets more pitches in than anybody. It all depends on the room.

The Co-Exec will be expected to have experience on set, making sure the director is getting the shots they need, and in post (editing) as well, since they may be filling in for the showrunner when necessary.

Salaries based on the WGA Series Compensation Guide:
Median salary: $25k to $27.5k per episode
Maximum salary: $55k per episode

CONSULTING PRODUCER

The consulting producer is usually a high-level writer who has an overall deal with the studio or network.

Overall Deals: Contracts that studios and networks sign with writers they want to work with in developing TV shows. These writers are paid a large salary to create shows for the studio and occasionally to work in a writers' room for one of the studio's shows. The upper echelon of writers on overall deals (Ryan Murphy, Shonda Rhimes, etc.) operate within their own worlds at their network or streamer and are not forced to write on anyone else's show.

Many of these writers have previously created and run shows of their own. Though their main focus is developing TV shows for the studio or network, they may be contracted to be placed as a writer on one of the studio's shows for two or three days a week. These writers can give a burst of much-needed experience and a veteran voice to the room.

However, not all consulting producers are on overall deals. There are plenty of others who are simply upper-level writers who don't want to or can't be there every day of the week. In other instances, they may also hold a specific technical skill or knowledge that's important to the show and are there more literally in a consulting role to assist the writers' room.

THE SHOWRUNNER/EXECUTIVE PRODUCER

The executive producer (EP), or at least one of them, is the showrunner, and is often the person who developed or created the show. These are the writer names you've likely heard of, such as Vince Gilligan, Aaron Sorkin, Shonda Rhimes, Larry David, Tina Fey, Chuck Lorre, and Mindy Kaling. This person is in control of the show and is in effect in charge of the entire production. There are line producers who handle the finances and the day-to-day of the production logistics, but the creative direction, writing, filming, and editing are all overseen by the showrunner.

The flow of a writers' room is completely dictated by a showrunner. When a room touches on an interesting topic that the showrunner wants to explore, they will guide the discussion in that direction. The showrunner will assign specific episodes to each writer, decide on the arc of the season, and even determine when the room starts and ends each day. During shooting, nothing can move forward unless the showrunner, or their proxy, has signed off on a scene, and all editing is approved by the showrunner before being sent to the network or studio.

The showrunner also sets the tone for the room. Some can be argumentative or abusive, which can make for a writers' room full of scared, angry writers. Some can be kind and freewheeling, creating a fun environment where writers are free to openly share ideas.

The best mix is a showrunner who knows what they want from the room—and asks for it—but also lets a room breathe and doesn't have to exert toxic energy to emphasize what they want. In my experience, I've found an important factor is whether the showrunner has a family they enjoy spending time with or a happy home life in general. Far too often, these career-obsessed showrunners have the opposite and would much prefer keeping the room at the office until the sun comes up to find a new angle on a story, rather than spend another night at home. I know that sounds sad, and I'm speaking purely from conjecture, but I'm also speaking from having experiences with eighteen different showrunners. Those who actually wanted to have a life outside the office were truly amazing to work for.

Salaries based on the WGA Series Compensation Guide:
Median salary for Executive Producers: $35k to $40k per episode
Median salary for Showrunners/Executive Producers: $42.5k to $52.5k per episode
Maximum showrunner salary: $175k per episode

CHAPTER 5

THE LIFE OF AN EPISODE

Successful writers tend to hone what they're good at and flex that muscle at the appropriate time. If you're a stand-up comedian and don't necessarily see "story" as one of your strengths, you're going to want to come in hard with jokes whenever the opportunity presents itself. Likewise, if you're good with character, story, or dialogue, you'll get your chance to flex those muscles in the writers' room at the appropriate times. Each of these skills is needed throughout the course of an episode's life cycle as it goes in and out of the writers' room.

As an aspiring TV writer, it's important to know the different stages a writers' room goes through in creating an episode from beginning to completion, starting from a kernel of an idea, and ending with shooting the episode. And if you're looking for a way to structure the creation of your own scripts, this will give some insight into how you can slowly build an idea out into a full script while slowly shaping and perfecting the story along the way.

BLUE SKY

Ah, the start of a writers' room—when highly paid professionals are reduced to schoolchildren, forced to sit together at the same table and figure out who the cool kids are going to be. It's an awkward time where people who were strangers moments before now must face each other and make conversation for eight hours a day—at minimum. But eventually everyone hits a groove and actually gets to work. The work during the first few weeks or months of pre-production is called Blue Sky.

First of all, what is pre-production? This is the time before the show starts to shoot. Many shorter-season cable and streaming shows will now schedule to have their entire season written before starting to shoot. Whether that's the case or not, at the start of a writers' room, only the pilot will have been written or sometimes even shot. Other than that, the room is starting from scratch. Sometimes writers are asked to send in a few story ideas. Other times, the showrunner will come in with story ideas they'd like to hit during the season. These days, with shorter seasons, showrunners will have a specific idea of where they want the season to go. In this case, the "Blue Sky" time in a writers' room, which I'll explain shortly, is skipped. Still, it's a helpful process for episodes that are still only bare-bones.

For rooms in which there is no sense of where the season is going to go, this is the most freewheeling time. Everything and anything is thrown at the wall to see what sticks. Story arcs are generated, larger character arcs are figured out, the tone begins to crystallize, and a season starts to come together.

The pitches during this time tend to veer away from dialogue and (in the case of sitcoms) jokes. Discussions are much more focused on stories and what to do with the characters. Sometimes, themes are being explored for what type of season this is going to be.

This tends to be a relaxed time in the writers' room. There are usually no late nights. This is when you're saying to yourself "Life is good. I get in at 10 a.m., leave by 5 p.m., and I have interesting conversations all day." It seems like things are going well and you might actually get ahead and have some episodes fully written before crunch time. And you really believe these things. But then the rest of the season happens, and everything goes haywire.

BREAKING OUT THE EPISODES

Once the general character and story arcs are laid out, the room gets down to figuring out what the actual episodes will be. The "Blue Sky" talk becomes much more focused, and the room narrows down the story into individual episodes, which are assigned to specific writers. So, even though all the writers are still discussing story ideas, one writer is taking a lead on that particular episode. Through lots of writing on a whiteboard and tinkering with different story beats, the general episode structure is decided upon. The writer of the episode will then pitch the story through to the room as a final way of seeing if anything is still not feeling quite right and making sure everybody's on the same page. Once the showrunner gives the okay, the writer begins working on the Story Area.

STORY AREA

The Story Area is the first piece in a long series of hurdles necessary to jump through to satisfy the studio and network. It is a two- to five-page document written in prose (in other words, not in script form) that summarizes that episode's story. The episode is not yet split into scenes. Instead, a general overview of the main storylines is laid out. Once the writer is finished with the Story Area, they'll send it back to the showrunner for final tweaks, then it's off to the studio. The studio gives their notes, then it's off to the network. The network gives their notes—the writer revises it and sends it back to them—and then finally, FINALLY it's time for the Outline. Oh, you thought you'd be writing a script by now?

It's important to note that this is the longest version of how episodes are written. Usually, the studio stops giving notes during the second season, leaving it solely to the network. But for at least the first few episodes of the first season, there are a lot of cooks in the kitchen.

OUTLINE

The Outline is an eight- to ten-page, detailed . . . well . . . outline of the episode. It is split into scenes, and it contains the story moves and emotions of each scene. In other words, the outline gives a genuine feel for the episode. When reading through the outline, the reader will be able to note the dramatic moments, the humorous moments, and feel how the individual scenes move the flow of the story along. At this point in the process, important dialogue or jokes are added. The outline serves as a last line of defense to identify any story or character problems that need to be fixed before writing the script. As with the previous step, the outline will go to the studio for notes, and then to the network for notes. Once approved, the writer is off on script.

Off on Script: A writer has been sent away from the writers' room by the showrunner to work on writing their episode.

WRITING THE EPISODE

At this stage, the writer gathers all the notes that have been taken in the room by the writers' assistant and no longer reports to the room every day. Instead, they are given a week or two during which they can focus all their attention on writing the script. Sometimes the writer doesn't need to come into the office at all. They can write to their heart's content all day, or putz around the whole week and write it really quickly at the last minute.

What I've described up until now is the way the flow of a room is supposed to work. And for rooms that write all their episodes before starting production, it usually does. But for shows that are under a strict deadline and have to write scripts while simultaneously filming episodes (which is the case on most network TV shows), the situation can devolve quickly.

For network shows, the "ideal system" holds up for the first four or five episodes. But then the studio has too many notes or the network throws out an episode they don't like and suddenly there's no time to send somebody off to write their own script. Instead, scripts are split off into scenes and various writers are sent to their offices for a couple of hours to write them. Or, in comedy rooms, sometimes a script is group-written. This is when the writers' assistant or script coordinator pulls up the script on the TV screen in the writers' room and types out the still-unformed script as dictated by the showrunner and other higher-ups.

ROOM/SHOWRUNNER REWRITE

Let's assume everything is still going well, and the writer has come back from being "off on script" with a completed episode. This is a stressful time for a writer because their script is about to be scrutinized by the showrunner or possibly the entire writers' room. Sometimes it goes well; sometimes it's tough to watch.

When I was a PA, I asked to sit in on the writers' room of the show I was working on. My very first day happened to be the day a mid-level writing team was turning in their script, and the showrunner did not like it. I sat next to the writers' assistant, who was diligently taking notes, as the showrunner tore into the writers. "You actually think this is good?!" "What were you even thinking?!" The two writers were reduced to puddles, and I for some reason decided to continue pursuing the goal of being a berated TV writer.

Other times, in less chaotic rooms, the writers praise bits of dialogue, or new character moves that better complement the larger story. This can be a productive, supportive, and collaborative moment.

Whatever the reaction may be, the script is then handed off to the showrunner, who will make changes before handing it off to the network or streamer.

In comedy rooms, alternatively, the script may be put up on two big TV screens in the writers' room and everyone will go through and make changes together. To an insecure writer, this part of the process is tantamount to a public flogging, as their finely tuned words are on display for all their peers, who subsequently change their words because they weren't good or funny enough, or so it feels. Now, most writers know that this is the nature of the beast and everybody's script gets changed and rewritten and it's no comment on the quality; but for those who are self-conscious of their writing—which, who isn't?—it can be brutal.

During this time in the room, people are really flexing their respective joke or story muscles. As opposed to the "before script" time, when all this story and script stuff was abstract, now there is actual material to work with, and the room can clearly see what is and is not working. Most of the time, this is no fault of the writer of the script. These were problems that were going to become evident whenever a fully fleshed-out script was written. In fact, many seasoned writers come to the room prepared with fixes for the issues that appeared as they were writing.

PUNCH-UP (EXCLUSIVE TO COMEDY)

In sitcoms, while the script is being rewritten, there's often a "joke room" or "alt room" that is broken off from the main writers' room. This room is full of the good joke writers and the lower-level writers to focus on one thing—making the script funnier. The showrunner will highlight a few areas or specific lines to work on throughout the script, and the group will go through these areas and come up with ten to twenty alternate jokes ("alts") for each one. The alts are then brought back to the showrunner and higher-ups, and the favorites are selected for the script.

SHOOTING THE EPISODE

At this point, the script has been written and it is now time to shoot it. From the writers' perspective, what's involved with shooting an episode depends on what type of show you're working on. While there has been a huge increase in content led primarily by streamers, recently we've also seen budget-cutting when it comes to a writer's tenure within a season of TV. Therefore, many current shows will have writers' rooms write all the episodes, and then only the showrunner or the showrunner and a couple of higher-level writers will remain for the shooting. This was a major source of contention during the 2023 negotiations between the WGA (the writers' union) and the AMPTP (the labor group representing the studios and producers). The WGA argued that writers are being cut out of the process and are losing a critical path to becoming knowledgeable showrunners. More on that later.

The writer of the episode is sometimes invited to set, and their role depends on what the showrunner is looking for. They may want somebody to bounce ideas off of, or they may want somebody to take the lead. But in this new world of shorter seasons and smaller writer budgets, you may not even be around for the shooting of your episode.

That being said, there are still places like network TV shows, where the traditional schedule is still followed. Episodes are shot as others are being written, and the writer is still involved during production. Episodes usually take a week to shoot, and what that week looks like greatly depends on whether you're working on a drama, a single-cam comedy, or a multi-cam comedy.

Dramas and Single-Cam Comedies

It all starts with a table read and a production meeting. During the table read, the writers and executives come into a room—usually stocked with a bunch of great snacks—and watch the actors perform the episode while sitting around a table. The writers will see what works and what doesn't work. When a table read goes well, you can feel the excited energy in the room. When a table read doesn't go well, you can also feel it, and it is uncomfortable. Like, "try to slip out of the room, pretending there's an emergency" uncomfortable. But there's usually eggs, bacon, and pastries. So even a bad table read isn't *that* bad.

The writers will then make any final changes to the script in the week or two before the production week begins. The writer of the episode and the showrunner will also attend a production, or tone, meeting, in which the director and all the heads of the production departments (lighting, costumers, set decoration, props, etc.) will go through the script and ask for details and/or guidance on each scene.

During the week an episode is being shot, the writer of the episode, a high-level writer, or the showrunner will be on set to make sure they're getting everything they need out of the shoot.

There are of course huge expensive series like *Game of Thrones* that are beasts unto themselves and do things their own way. What I'm describing applies to the majority of TV shows that *don't* operate under a gigantic feature film budget.

Multi-Cam Comedies

Multi-cams are traditional sitcoms. In fact, all TV was multi-cam for decades, but today only a select few network shows and even fewer streaming shows are. If you think of multi-cam comedies as a dying medium, as many do, feel free to skip ahead. For everyone else, I've included a scheduled production week that is standard across multi-cams and has been around for decades. If you're interested in this type of comedy or the history of comedy in general, read on!

Production weeks are very intense for multi-cams because every day in the week leads up to a show night when the audience is loaded in and nearly the whole show is taped in one sitting. In

THE LIFE OF AN EPISODE 51

the days leading up to the taping, the writers are refining the script, while each day seeing the latest version of the script performed by the actors on set like a stage play. And for much of the recent history of TV multi-cams, the name ubiquitous with sitcoms was director Jimmy Burrows. (If you don't know this name, look him up. He's directed episodes of every single sitcom you've ever heard of for the last fifty years.)

Since the weeks are so formally structured, here is what a production week looks like at a typical multi-cam:

DAY 1: TABLE READ DAY

Much like with dramas and single-cams, the actors all gather around a table and perform the script in front of the writers, the crew, and the executives.

After the table read, the network and studio execs leave to confer in a separate room. This is an existential moment for the writers, because the next twenty minutes will dictate how the rest of the week will go. If the network comes back with "Great! Just a few page notes," maybe you can make those after-work plans. If they come back with "We're just not really understanding . . ." you can call your friends, family, or casual hook-up and tell them "Sorry, maybe next week."

While the actors and the director go down to stage and start to work out their blocking, the writers return to the room and get to work.

Blocking: A directing term referring to the moves the actors will make during their scenes. Since the cameras, the sound, and the viability of the scene depend on everyone being coordinated, the blocking is important to establish who's walking where, who comes into the scene when, and generally what the scene will look like on set.

The writers' room convenes, the writers' assistant and script co-ordinator put the script up on the big screen, and they start making changes. (I will get into this more in the assistant section, but in these comedy writers' rooms, there are always big TV screens in the room, and the writers' assistant or script coordinator makes changes to the script as dictated by the showrunner.) The changes are made, hopefully by a reasonable hour, and a new draft of the script goes out to everyone.

DAY 2: WRITERS' RUN-THROUGH

Equipped with blue scripts in hand (which denotes the first revised script of the episode), the writers flock to the stage and immediately go right to crafty.

Crafty: Short for craft services. These are the snacks and meals that are put out on stages or sets that are free for all. If you're lucky, a run-through will coincide with stage lunch time, so you can have your choice of your writer's lunch or the stage lunch. These are the big decisions that made up the majority of my thinking power as an assistant, which may very well have added to my years as an assistant.

A run-through is like watching the episode, but in a small group standing directly in front of the stage. At the writers' run-through, only the writers and the stage crew are present; and with such a small group, jokes that fall flat really fall flat. Any blocking, jokes, dialogue, or story that isn't working is painfully evident. In fact, if anybody after the table read still had not called and canceled their evening plans, they are now running out to do just that—babysitters are booked, therapy is rescheduled, and significant others are being pissed off.

After a conference with the director, the writers head to the writers' room and discuss what needs to change. Once again, the script is put up on the big screen and the writers make changes.

DAY 3: NETWORK/STUDIO RUN-THROUGH

Now that all hope is lost for having a good week, the writers saunter over to the stage with pink scripts in hand, denoting a second revised script. After ravaging crafty, everyone settles in for a much more crowded run-through than the day before. This time the network and studio execs are present. Once again, the episode is run through, sometimes with music interludes played as the actors move between sets, in an attempt to keep the energy up and convince the execs they're having a good time.

Usually there is marked improvement day over day, and hope returns that maybe, just maybe, tonight won't be like every other night and you'll be able to go home early. The execs confer in their room and eventually, like kings and queens, the showrunners are sent for by the Assistant Director. "The execs are awaiting you in their chambers." The notes are given and the writers complete the rewrite. At the end of the day, a Shooting Draft of the script is distributed. That means the hoops have been jumped through and it is time to begin putting the project on film, or video, or whatever they shoot things with these days. I don't know, I'm a writer.

DAY 4: PRE-SHOOTS

While the rest of the room begins work on the next episode, the writer of the current week's script—or an upper-level writer—remains on stage during pre-shoots. Pre-shoots are scenes deemed by production to be too complicated to shoot on show night. They are typically scenes that involve a stunt or a wardrobe change, are hard for the audience to see because they're in the back of the studio, or they're integral to the storyline and they want to make sure they get a few cracks at it.

During pre-shoots, the actors perform to nobody but the crew and have to time their lines to accommodate for the eventual laugh, which will be provided on show night when these scenes are shown to the live audience on a video screen.

To help with the timing, sometimes "paid laughers" are hired. I have seen and done my fair share of miserable Hollywood jobs, but this one takes the cake. "Paid laughers" consist of a group of twenty to thirty people scattered among the audience, paid to come in and laugh at punch lines so the actors can get their rhythm. It's well-intentioned, but the result is a scary dissonant laughter that isn't quite loud enough to be pleasant in the cavernous stages. Instead, it becomes creepy, horror movie laughter and is completely out of sync with what's happening on stage. Overheard quote from the Assistant Director: "Can somebody tell the laughers they're laughing at the set-up and not the punch line?"

DAY 5: SHOW NIGHT

After a day of writing, the writers head down to the stage at 5 p.m. The audience is loaded in, the cast is introduced, and the show is filmed. Depending on the showrunner, this can be a relaxing time for the writers, where they may be called on once or twice to come up with a different joke or alternate line for one that's not working. But during show nights with a more demanding showrunner, writers are required to huddle up after every scene while the showrunner—screaming to be heard over the candy-fueled audience and music to keep everyone pumped up between takes—tasks the writers with pitching different lines and jokes for the actors as quickly as possible.

Meanwhile, the audience has an MC and DJ for the night who has started getting the energy of the crowd up long before the show starts to tape. One show I worked on for two years had the same warm-up guy every week. He was great and kept the audience entertained and hyped and full of candy with the exact same routine each time. Judging solely by what joke he was telling or what song was playing, I could tell you how close we were to being wrapped for the night. Another warm-up act had a "ladder on the chin while riding a very tall unicycle" trick in his repertoire. It was harrowing, and the whole crew and writers and actors would come out to watch. Great warm-up acts get the audience pumped up and laughing hard, which means only minor sweetening is needed afterwards, or sometimes none at all.

Sweetening: Adjusting laughs in post-production for a multi-cam sitcom with a live audience. In the 1950s, Charles Douglass invented the Laff Box, a physical box with pre-recorded laughs that he would bring to editors of various sitcoms to add laughter when needed. He kept the box under lock and key and carefully protected its engineering, but eventually new engineers entered the laugh-sweetening space.

On a good night, shooting wraps around 8 or 9 p.m. On a bad night, the bleary-eyed writers and crew stumble out of the stage at 1 or 2 a.m., and get ready for the table read the next morning to repeat this same week all over again for the following episode.

CHAPTER 6

PILOTS

Throughout TV history, almost all shows began with a pilot. A pilot is the first episode of any show, and it's usually produced before the TV show is ordered to series. See, networks and streamers are all about hedging their bets. Before committing to a season of a TV show, they'll shoot just the pilot episode. If it goes well and it receives a good reaction from their test audiences, they move forward and order episodes. Other pilots that don't fare as well in the testing phase never see the light of day. Even though pilots are slowly being replaced by mini-rooms (which I'll get to shortly), they are still a major part of many TV shows' life cycles.

Pilots provide a unique opportunity for newcomers to prove themselves and possibly get hired on the show if it goes to series. Because pilots are a bit of a testing ground, there are many more pilots made than there are TV series. And the assistant jobs on these shows can give you a way in. I worked on many TV pilots, most of which did not move forward and become a series, but they did provide an opportunity to meet people and eventually get hired when my bosses moved on to a different show.

Traditionally, all pilots on broadcast networks happened in the exact same season . . . pilot season. This happened in the spring, and there would be a mad scramble to staff up, cast, and shoot a pilot in about a month. However, that system has changed. Streamers do not abide by a strict TV season model, and most broadcast networks now have a rolling schedule for picking up new TV shows.

Traditional Broadcast TV Season: TV history buffs, listen up. This is a layout of a traditional season of broadcast TV. The pilot season, as mentioned, would happen in early spring. In May, the network "upfronts" would take place, when the new fall TV shows were unveiled to advertisers. This is when you found out which pilots were picked up and which ones died a horrible death. Networks would then give TV shows that made the cut a thirteen-episode order. They would start the writers' room in the summer, and they would wrap up by the winter holidays. And all this time, productions are waiting to hear if they've gotten their "back nine," which is the continuation of the season, making for a full twenty-two episodes. If they don't get the "back nine," cancellation is imminent. A version of this system is still in place to a much more limited extent with broadcast networks.

Pilots can be stressful, as the showrunner has to perfect the script—which the network and/or studio will have copious notes on—without an official writers' room. Instead, showrunners will call on their writer friends. This provides an opportunity for writers who are not currently employed in a writers' room. They will bounce from pilot to pilot to pitch on story or jokes, sometimes because they've been asked to as a favor, sometimes because they're a burgeoning assistant who has asked to come in (that was me), and sometimes because a writer's agent wants them to get in that room and meet people. The result is an awkward mix of friends and desperate people (that was me) in a situation that turns into a bit of an "on the job" interview. If the pilot gets picked up to series, the showrunner will have slots to fill. And it helps anybody looking for a job to have pitched or contributed to that show getting picked up during a particularly stressful time for the showrunner.

For assistants looking to get their foot in the door, pilots are such a mad scramble that production teams are more likely to take a chance on unproven assistants because they need a whole staff of people, and they need them now. This was how I landed one of my first writers' assistant jobs. I was very green, but the team was desperate, and I was a nice enough guy. But TV pilot jobs are never advertised, so you need to have some previous connections to get in. Even though it's just a month of work, it can be extremely beneficial in the long term. I was a script coordinator on a pilot that ended up getting ordered to series, and it was on that show that I wrote my second episode of network TV, which got me into the WGA.

There were also pilots I worked on that did not go to series and still proved helpful. In fact, one pilot was so bad that it didn't even finish shooting. Following a disastrous network run-through, we were supposed to meet the network executives in the green room and get notes. But the network executives weren't there. In fact, they hated the run-through so much that they left right away and sent an email that the show was canceled. They hated it so much that they couldn't even wait until the next day when it was going to be shot to cancel it. (And can I tell you something? They were right.) And *still*, even in the most monumentally disastrous of circumstances, I made connections that would lead to jobs for years to come.

CHAPTER 7

STREAMING AND MINI-ROOMS

THE STREAMING REVOLUTION

Streaming has completely changed the TV industry. Cable channels and networks used to operate on a strict seasonal model for shooting pilots and beginning and ending their productions. Streamers decided they were no longer going to do it that way, and networks and cable channels were forced to follow suit. Previously, networks were continuously pumping out twenty-two-episode seasons of TV shows, while cable shows would go for thirteen episodes. Streamers came along and said we're doing however many we want. The network TV business model is to have a show last for enough seasons that it becomes a hit and sells into syndication. The new subscription model for streamers focuses more on a large array of TV shows rather than large numbers of seasons and episodes.

We get it, things are different. Why does this matter? The implications of these changes are being felt far and wide across the industry, and, more importantly for our purposes, in the writers' room. Most of these changes have both positives and a lot of negatives, many of which were at the heart of the WGA writers' strike in 2023.

The archaic system of TV shows all beginning at one specific time of the year is one of the most important positive outcomes of the changes brought about by streaming. In the past, if you didn't have a job come September, you were looking at a long cold winter without work. In fact, unless you got lucky, you were probably going to be waiting until early spring before you could hopefully find work on a pilot. Now shows are staffing writers and assistants all year round.

Adding to this boon for TV job seekers is the fact that there are more shows than ever before. Content is king, and in the past few years the streamers have been racing for more and more of it for their platforms. Every day there's a new flash-in-the-pan show that somebody is recommending you watch, adding yet another series to the ever-growing list of TV you need to be well versed in to stay relevant in social situations. More recently, the streamers have seen their subscriber counts diminish, so this unchecked open-faucet valve of spending is on its last legs. Still, the fact remains, there are more shows than ever before. And this should mean more *jobs* than ever before too, right? Well, sort of . . .

In this intense push for more content, the money has gone to production budgets and high-level talent. And by that, I don't necessarily mean the most talented people. I'm referring to the recognizable actors on screen and the higher-level writers in the writers' rooms. The common refrain when hunting for a TV writing job these days is "it's a small room, only upper levels." Internal TV operating budgets are getting squeezed, and those being neglected are the writers at the bottom of the ladder. Writers' rooms are becoming small operations filled with already-experienced writers, not allowing for much growth for lower- and mid-level writers.

The time spent in writers' rooms is also waning. In the cable and streaming world, oftentimes the showrunner and maybe one or two upper-level writers are the only ones to remain on staff for production after the writers' room is wrapped. And any person who's worked in TV can tell you, things change when shooting, and it's helpful for a showrunner to have a room of writers to support them when episodes undoubtedly need to be rewritten. Even editing is a form of writing. Stories are still being molded. The last rewrite is still taking place.

But this shouldn't affect the assistants, right? It sure does. While there are more opportunities than ever to find a job, the jobs don't last very long. In the old network days, if you got a job, you could generally count on being employed for nine months. But this new model is turning the entire TV landscape into a gig economy, so assistants and writers can never be complacent or feel secure in their jobs. For assistants, it greatly impacts your ability to make deeper connections and move up, which I'll get into more in the section on assistant jobs.

MINI-ROOMS

Remember when I said that networks and streamers like to hedge their bets? This is the ultimate bet hedge. As the avalanche of content increases, networks and streamers alike have sought ways to cut costs. Eliminating pilots is one of the ways streamers found to do that. Instead, they make use of mini-rooms, or development rooms.

A mini-room is a small group of usually upper-level writers assembled to work on a TV show. But unlike a regular writers' room, this show has not yet been greenlit.

Greenlight: When a network greenlights a TV show, they have decided to move forward and produce the show.

Instead of making a pilot and deciding then whether or not they'll make the show, streamers will bring together a mini-room to write multiple episodes, or sometimes an entire season of the show. If the streamer decides they like the episodes, they'll greenlight the series. Only then will the show enter production, during which only a few upper-level writers will remain on staff.

By setting up mini-rooms, streamers—and now some net-works—can eliminate costly writers' rooms altogether and, unfor-tunately, create fewer opportunities for lower-level writers to get their foot in the door.

There are legitimate reasons to have a mini-room, such as flesh-ing out a series idea that still needs development or creating a deeper established mythology for shows that require a decent amount of world-building. However, on the whole, it's become a money-saving practice.

CHAPTER 8

HOW TO BEHAVE IN
A WRITERS' ROOM

It might seem counterintuitive to include a chapter on how to behave in a writers' room following story after story of the most ridiculous work behavior imaginable. That being said, certain qualities and ways of approaching speaking and pitching in the room will make you stand out as a collaborative, creative person, whereas other qualities will do precisely the opposite. Now, there are also times when rooms are so toxic and filled with such bad behavior that your well-intentioned approach won't matter anyway. Later, I'm going to talk about how to manage those situations in addition to which types of rooms to avoid entirely.

CHOOSING WHEN AND HOW MUCH TO SPEAK

For now, let's pretend all is well in the writers' room. You're a new writer, or a writers' assistant who's spoken to the showrunner and gotten permission to pitch, and you want to make a good impression. But you're not sure when to speak. The conversation is moving at a fast clip. You don't want to talk more than you should, but you also don't want to be silent. On top of that, some rooms insist on unspoken hierarchies in which writers are expected to speak in an amount according to their title. That's why, when entering a new room, it's best to gauge the next level writer up from you, see how much they're pitching, and mimic their frequency. They can't fault you if you're a staff writer and you're speaking as much as the story editor. But if you're talking as much as a co-executive producer or the showrunner, you should probably chill out for a few weeks until you get a feel for the room. Every room is different, and you will feel out your role within it quickly. But at first, while you're still figuring out the dynamics, this is a safe way to play it.

FIGHTING FOR YOUR PITCH

Okay, you've spoken up, said your pitch, and somebody has disagreed. And maybe that person is the showrunner, so you're up against your boss. If you don't feel that strongly about the pitch, let it go. But if you do feel that this is important for the show, here's how to approach it. The general rule is that you get two more cracks at it. The second time, you can reiterate your point, present it in a slightly different way, and explain why this is important. If it gets shot down again, then you're playing with fire. But if it's important to you and you *really* need to get your point across, you can give an "I'm sorry, I'm going to pitch this one more time and then I'll drop it, but it's really important to me that . . ." This shows that you're aware that you're harping on the same point, and you feel it's important enough to pitch again. Now, there are certain times when the rule doesn't matter, such as if information in a script is false or a line of dialogue is culturally insensitive. These you should feel okay bringing up all day long. But for strong differences of opinion, three-strikes-and-you're-out is a good approach.

WHAT MAKES A GREAT PITCH

Now let's talk about the actual pitch—the idea you're presenting to the group. This can either be a one-line joke in a comedy or a complex character storyline that affects the episode or season. Whatever you're pitching, it should be well thought out. I know that sounds obvious, but there's a subtlety to it that a lot of writers don't fully understand. This means you can't speak up with "What if this character says 'how's it going,' and the other character has a joke . . ." It means you can't pitch "Maybe John should break into the hideout, guns blazing, and then something happens, and he gets arrested . . ." Both of these are half-ideas—meaning it's requiring the room to step in and finish what you've started. So, instead of providing a solution, which is all the showrunner is looking for, you've actually presented more problems.

But isn't it a collaborative environment? Aren't all ideas acceptable? Sometimes. There may be a time in a writers' room when a particular plot point is giving everyone trouble. And maybe a fresh framework could shake things up. In that case, it's perfectly okay to say "Is it all right if I pitch a general area?" or something to that effect. That way, the room is aware that you know you're not providing a pitch, just an interesting idea that may help the room break through whatever's holding them back. However, that should only be employed when it's clear that the room is at an impasse. Because more than anything, it's important to follow the flow of the room.

When a room is really moving, dialogue, story ideas, and character moves flow easily. A good showrunner will follow the direction a story is going and will dictate where to go next. That's why it's so important to follow the showrunner's lead and not go backwards. Rooms that are in the zone can be turned upside-down by somebody saying "Can we go back for a second?" This could happen because a problem has been noticed in a previous act. But unless that issue completely kills the rest of the story, or contributes to a Nakamura, it can be fixed later. Stopping a room kills momentum and makes it harder to restart and get the flow of the room moving again.

Nakamura: A joke or story point that fails in the beginning of the episode, causing all further references to die along with it. The story goes that the term came from an episode of *Taxi* where a character discussed a car part from a Japanese company named Nakamura. The joke died, and every subsequent reference and callback to it, of which there were many, died along with it.

Be confident in your pitch. Many writers will begin their pitches with "I don't know if this works, but ..." or, "Not this, but ..." and it kills the enthusiasm for your idea. It puts the pitch on shaky footing before it's even been said. People will immediately look for reasons why it won't work, because you've told them "What I'm about to say is going to be problematic."

BEING IGNORED

Okay, you're using the best writers' room etiquette, you're picking the right time to speak and being respectful of the flow of the room, and yet people are ignoring you. Sometimes this will happen. I've spent many hours as a script coordinator behind a computer with people ignoring my pitches, or ignoring the fact that I'm speaking altogether, simply because the assistant in the corner isn't supposed to be talking. There's also the all-too-present phenomenon of ideas being heard, slightly reworded, and presented as their own generally by higher-level male writers who've heard an idea they liked from a female writer. This is why I'm a fan of fostering a "credit-giving" environment.

When you know you're using a piece of someone else's idea for your pitch, use a "bouncing off of what [writer who was being ignored] was saying" to frame your pitch. This keeps that person in the game. Also, if you hear an idea being taken and repurposed as their own, feel free to call it out. It doesn't have to be offensive. It can be as simple as "Right, that was a great pitch by [ignored writer]."

Of course, stealing someone else's idea is unacceptable, and being nice clearly won't force assholes to not be assholes. But this kind of "credit-giving" environment can change the dynamic of a room. It's not every person out for themselves. Instead, it's a team effort.

The biggest offenders will not be changing any time soon. But if the others in a room are together in calling out the rightful pitcher of an idea, the offenders will be put on their toes, and will have to be more careful in the future. It's also impossible to speak up in a room for your own pitch and say "Hey, that was my idea." It just doesn't have the right impact, as people could misconstrue it as selfish. But people coming in to defend your ideas, and you coming in to defend theirs, are selfless and devoid of perceived narcissism. If I didn't have well-respected people in writers' rooms saying "What was that pitch?" and giving me the floor, or giving me credit where credit was due, I would not have been recognized and I would never have gotten my first chance to write a script.

These tips can be helpful to keep in mind even outside the writers' room. Maybe you're in a writers' group or you're working with some friends on a short film. Establishing this type of brainstorming behavior and uplifting environment will make the whole process easier and more fun.

TOXIC ROOMS: BEHAVIOR AND TRAITS TO LOOK OUT FOR

The etiquette I previously outlined is how to operate in a writers' room that still has hope and where there's still a bit of professional decency. But a television season is a difficult thing to get through. Even if you enjoy the people you work with, you are still expending a tremendous amount of effort over extremely long days. And sometimes this brings out the worst in people. Other times, the people in the writers' room are simply terrible.

Some discussions/statements I've overheard from writers during a long season:

- Discussions of Ativan and Xanax prescription dosages
- Wondering whether it's possible to comfortably sleep in the office
- Annoyance at a different TV show office next door that sounded like they were having more fun than we were
- Marry, screw, kill—three other writers who were all present
- How they would kill the network executives

Writers' rooms can be cruel. I've seen people brought to tears, harassed, made fun of, and get into screaming matches with each other. I've seen lots of racism and lots of sexism. The problem is that it's hard not to be yourself when you're in a room for twelve hours a day, five days a week, for nine months. And sometimes our real selves are terrible people.

But how can situations get that bad? Isn't there oversight? Yes, technically there is. But it's never really clear who is doing the overseeing. And that starts with the fact that on major TV productions, it's not always obvious who you're working for. Writers and assistants are hired by the show's production, which is renting space from the studio. And though the studio is paying the production to make the show, they are also renting studio space to them. So, TV productions and studios are both clients and customers. But no matter where the money is coming from, the assistants are paid through a third-party company anyway—a company called Entertainment Partners (it's almost always them), who will always get some tax thing wrong that will become painfully and frustratingly hard to deal with, come April 15. Then there are the smaller production companies that the studios have under them operating as subsidiaries that are technically producing the shows. That's not even to mention the network the show is airing on. With all these different entities at play, when it comes down to it, I'm not even sure who I've technically worked for on all these television productions. Yes, I worked on *2 Broke Girls*, which aired on CBS. But was my employer the *2 Broke Girls* production? Was it Warner Bros.? Was it Entertainment Partners, the folks who gave me my checks? Or was it Bonanza Productions, a WB subsidiary? I have no idea!

In addition, if someone were to go to the studio's HR, there's a big question regarding where the HR loyalties lie. It's not likely to be with the lowly assistant who has been working there a few months. It's probably with the showrunner/creator with the overall deal who they pay millions of dollars. (That's complete conjecture, but with everything that's come out in the past few years, maybe it isn't?) On top of that, writers and assistants alike are imbued with such a fight-or-flight scarcity mentality that you're encouraged not to rock the boat. Getting a reputation as somebody who's "hard to work with" can hurt your career, particularly when you're just starting out.

These dire words of warning are meant to scare, but these bad work situations are not universal. I've worked for as many toxic showrunners as I have for great showrunners who really cared and wanted to help. But honestly, 50/50 ain't great, and for many this behavior has been perpetuated and solidified over the years—even by the Supreme Court of California in partnership with Warner Bros. and that ever-so-charming TV show *Friends*.

Friends Law

Back in the '90s, a case was brought against the executive producers of *Friends* by a writers' assistant who was offended by some statements made in the writers' room. The court filings discuss lewd drawings, miming masturbation, and some other descriptions of sticks and twigs inside places that I just don't feel right putting in a book that I'm hoping students will read. The plaintiff argued that this fostered an inappropriate and abusive working environment.

The case was long-fought and went all the way to the Supreme Court of California. And Warner Bros., who was the studio producing *Friends* and the defendant in the case, won. The court ruled that coarse language was just par for the course in a "creative workplace."

This means that for years, writers reveled in a free-rein mentality that anything was okay to say and do in a writers' room. Okay, writers' rooms already operated under that assumption. But this put it in legalese. The ruling seemingly gave creative people carte blanche to act as they wished when operating under the guise of creativity. I've read about the case and what was said, and while it may sound surprising to someone who has not worked in TV, it's actually pretty tame compared to a lot of what is overheard in writers' rooms. And that's not to excuse the behavior at all. What I'm saying is the language can be rough. And it doesn't stop at language. The insecurity of being a writer, and the power given to showrunners can make some powerful people lose their minds, allowing manipulative, abusive, insulting behavior to run rampant.

It sounds dramatic, but this is necessary information for somebody who's looking to enter this environment.

But hasn't TV had its reckoning? Haven't the bad guys been outed? A few very high-level abusers have been thrown out. But there are plenty of abusive people still enjoying a great deal of success in the industry. Maureen Ryan's excellent book, *Burn It Down: Power, Complicity, and a Call for Change in Hollywood* (2023) is a fantastically terrifying reminder that these situations continue to this day. And even though *Burn It Down* is described as an exposé, many of these stories have been open secrets for years. The culprits have been allowed to continue their toxic, abusive, sexist, racist behavior because of companies who are loath to do anything to challenge their bottom lines.

THE GOOD ROOMS

Wooh, didn't think it would get that grim, did you? Well, don't despair. Not all rooms are like that. Rooms can be exciting and fun. Rooms can be positive and creative. And rooms can be an amazing learning experience for anybody who wants to understand TV and screenwriting structure.

Before spending time in a writers' room—first as a production assistant and later as a writers' assistant and script coordinator—I had no idea how a TV show was crafted. I thought a bunch of people assembled in a room, came up with cool ideas, and then wrote scripts. But it's the flow of the discussions, learning the correct time to speak, structuring and beating out story points, putting them on the board, pitching the stories, and understanding how the studio and network play into it all that I couldn't have learned anywhere else. Only being inside the writers' room could have given me these tools, and the stories, friends, connections, and experiences that came with them.

PART III

ASSISTANTING

People get into TV writing through a myriad of avenues, routes, careers, and connections. I want to make that very clear at the beginning of this section. Some begin by writing or directing movies or short films that catch somebody's attention. Others write plays or brave the stand-up comedy and improv scene. There are those who get in through workshops or contests, or through the agency or manager world where reps can make some calls and give someone a much-needed boost.

All of the aforementioned methods are perfectly viable ways to get into the TV writers' room, and I would recommend any of them. The thing is, it's very difficult to win writing contests, and it's very unlikely (based on numbers alone) that you'll get into a workshop. And any other route has its own hurdles and obstacles. I'm not saying you shouldn't pursue those options, but the assistant jobs I'm going to discuss can be used in tandem with other routes as a tool to meet people, to expand your network, and to make a name for yourself as a writer.

The following assistant jobs follow a trajectory in increasing levels of seniority. However, they do not represent a career path. While one job is supposed to lead to the next and eventually get you staffed on a TV show as a writer, it only works that way for a very small fraction of people. The idea of an assistant career path was established when shows lasted twenty-two episodes, and there were many, many seasons. These longer seasons and more stable jobs allowed time for everyone to get to know you, and it gave you a chance to move up the ladder in between seasons. With episode and season orders shrinking across the board, the "path" these jobs used to provide has all but been removed.

While you may not necessarily climb a career ladder in rung order, nor hold each of the positions discussed in this section, it's important for you to know that each of the assistant jobs in the writers' office holds its own benefits. And though you can't expect an easy ride to becoming a staff writer, these jobs can get you in the writers' room, they can get you a freelance script, and they can allow you to meet the person or people who can give you your break. These jobs also provide invaluable writing experience. You'll begin to understand what showrunners look for in a writer, and what execs are looking for in terms of the structure, characters, and dialogue in your scripts. My scripts sucked before I set foot in a writers' room. (Some would argue they still suck today.) But they unquestionably improved because of my time spent in the room.

Assistant jobs can also provide a starting point in the industry. Let's say you haven't won any competitions, you haven't gotten into any fellowships or workshops, you don't do stand-up, and Jordan Peele isn't your second cousin once removed. You can still meet people and claw your way into the industry as an assistant on a TV show.

An assistant job is also a good place to learn whether or not TV writing is something you want to do with your life. If you've been convincing yourself that you want to heal the world with a good story, a year as an assistant may disavow you of your good intentions. I've seen many people spend one season as a production assistant and then move out of LA. And I don't blame them. These can be really difficult jobs. But don't take my bluntness as a warning that assistant jobs are only for those who are strong enough to "tough it out." They will simply show you the reality of what it means to work on a TV show day to day, and it may not be your cup of tea. Or it may be exactly what you're looking for.

When I first arrived in LA, I was very unsure about the industry and whether I wanted to pursue TV writing. There was a lot of positive potential egging me on: the high writer salaries that could be in my future, the creative possibilities of being on the inside of creating a TV show—and there were many factors telling me to switch careers: my abysmal salary, the long hours, the toxic personalities. Then I got in as a writers' assistant on a supportive show. I pitched my first joke that made it into a script. I got to watch a TV legend speak my words. It made the edit and I got to watch my joke on national TV, an episode that was watched by over 5 million people. I got to write my first scene, then my first script. I got my name on the "written by" credits of a major network TV show. And all those amazing experiences happened while I was an assistant, and as a direct result of being an assistant. There are things I would have done differently in my career climb, but none of it would have been possible for me without some combination of assistant jobs and the contacts that came with them.

CHAPTER 9

GETTING YOUR FIRST JOB

Coming into the TV industry as a complete newbie can be daunting. It's difficult to know where to start your job hunt, or even what job to look for. So let's break down some of the mysteries behind getting your first job in the industry. Let's say you're looking to get your foot in the door, gain some experience, learn the landscape, make some connections, or, at the very least, determine if this industry is right for you. This chapter will focus on very practical ways to get started and provide you with websites and suggestions for places to search for your first job.

Regarding education, it should be noted that no college degrees are required for most entry-level jobs in the TV industry. And for the most part, no experience is required either. A lot of decisions will come down to whether or not people get a good impression from you. So, that's the good news about getting in; here's the bad news. Assistant jobs at major TV shows are not posted online. More often than not, the people hiring will simply ask their friends and coworkers if they know anybody for a certain position. There are no rules stating that a position must go up on a site to avoid nepotism or favoritism. The industry runs on nepotism and favoritism! Still, these jobs are attainable. And jobs at smaller production companies can help you make connections and lead to bigger shows at major studios.

The common refrain I heard when entering the industry and getting started was to "get a PA job." That's a nice idea, and it is the most common entryway into the industry. But how do you get that PA job? How do you get any assistant or entry-level job without knowing anybody or anything about the industry? Nothing beats simply meeting somebody who is looking for an assistant, or having a friend who knows somebody who's hiring. But you're new, you might not have those connections yet. So, the following are the various methods my friends, coworkers, and I have used to get our first assistant jobs. And while these are practical methods, you can also think of this as a way to fuel your own thinking about how to break in. More creative ways of getting jobs are certainly out there, and the job market is always evolving with new opportunities springing up every day.

ENTERTAINMENT JOB SITES

I got my first PA job in LA off Craigslist. Though the number of jobs on there has severely dwindled since that time, there are still a few advertised. Even my page job at *The Late Show with David Letterman*, though I was referred through a friend, was advertised on Craigslist. However, as a whole, the bigger studios' assistant jobs are not going to be found there. What you will find are smaller productions where you can learn the ropes and start meeting people. Of course, as with anything on Craigslist—from a stained mattress to a missed connection to a gently used toaster—take caution that it's not a scam.

There are a number of job sites specifically for entertainment industry jobs. Personally, I have had no luck with these, but they do work for some. These Indeed.com-style job sites have a particularly large number of production crew jobs:

- Mandy.com
- EntertainmentCareers.net
- StaffMeUp.com
- Showbizjobs.com

Most of these have some level of membership they want you to pay for in order to get the "premium" jobs, or whatever they call them. Most of the time that's not necessary. There are a lot of people applying to these jobs, but it's not unheard of to get an interview from these sites. If you're starting your hunt, then you should be blasting your résumé all over the place, and these sites are a good place to start.

The California Film Commission also has a website with links to entertainment job sites as well as diversity job training and placement services. There is some overlap with the sites mentioned above, but it's well worth checking out. You can find their list here: film.ca.gov/production/entertainment-jobs/

THE UTA JOB LIST/THE ANONYMOUS PRODUCTION ASSISTANT

Years ago, the United Talent Agency (UTA) began compiling a job list every couple of weeks that circulates throughout the industry. Jobs on the list include openings for lower-level positions such as executive assistant and production assistant, as well as development, agency, and management company positions. The UTA Job List is a bit of a crapshoot. Since everybody knows about it, everybody applies for the jobs on the list. There are stories on Screenwriting Reddit of assistants at production companies who have had to swim through the torrential downpour of applications and admit that, due to necessity, they stop after only a couple dozen and never even look at the rest. But if you have a résumé and a standard cover letter that you can tweak to match the right job, there's really no reason not to throw your hat in the ring.

These job postings also present a way you can gather valuable job-hunting information. You may be able to determine if somebody you know happens to know somebody, who happens to know somebody, who's somehow connected to those hiring. It might be a far-flung six degrees of separation. But knowing what's available could prompt you to consider who you can, and should, reach out to.

The UTA Job List used to be a bit easier to find. However, there's not many sites where it pops up on a semiweekly basis anymore. Therefore, The Anonymous Production Assistant (anonymousproductionassistant.com/uta-joblist) is a great place to look. It has been around for years and has lots of information about being a production assistant, in addition to the UTA Job List and other jobs that it posts on its own job board.

ALUMNI ASSOCIATIONS

There is of course a big "if" here. *If* you went to college or are in college, you likely have an alumni association. And it is likely there will be alumni who are connected to the entertainment industry in some form or another. It may not be the connection you're hoping for, like an executive producer at a huge TV show. But even a tangential connection can make a big difference. Alumni offices can connect graduates to successful alumni who have offered their help to up-and-comers. If colleges have a lot of alumni in a particular city, they may even throw networking events where you can increase your connections.

Another way to connect, which I've found helpful, are alumni-run Facebook and Google groups. For example, Syracuse University has a Google Group specifically for alumni who are working in production in LA. Those who apply to jobs posted on this group tend to get a much higher response rate, since they've already been vetted as an alum. Most colleges don't have the same volume of alumni working in the industry that Syracuse does, but maybe you're friends with somebody whose college has a great association and similar types of groups. If you can't get into it yourself, ask those friends to keep an eye out for whatever type of position you're looking for.

FACEBOOK & GOOGLE GROUPS

Facebook groups and Google Groups have been instrumental for networking, finding jobs, and also for outing bad behavior in the industry. There was one Facebook group in particular called Awesome Assistants that became a mainstay for information for job seekers, helpful hints about the industry, and even calling out toxic and abusive bosses and warning fellow assistants which jobs to stay away from. Its popularity spawned many different iterations of Awesome Assistants groups geared toward different niches in the industry.

There are also similar Facebook groups focused on specific jobs, like the "I need a . . ." series of Facebook groups. They include "I need a Production Assistant," "I need an editor," or "I need a production crew." They are lively and helpful but, unfortunately, like the Awesome Assistants groups, they are closed, meaning you need somebody to vouch for you or you need your first job in the industry in order to get in. There are always hurdles, but hey, you're resourceful.

Most of the Google Groups are also closed. However, once you get to the point where you're able to join, there is a Script Coordinator Google Group that is one of the few places I've seen script coordinator and writers' assistant jobs posted. They're also helpful for job disputes and salary information. Along this same line, there is an IATSE Local 871 group for script coordinators and writers' assistants. This is a group dedicated to the union that script coordinators and writers' assistants must join. I will go into this in more detail in the next chapter, but please note that these are not entry-level jobs, and you will probably not be able to get into these if you're just starting out. However, if you know a writers' assistant or script coordinator, you can ask that they keep a lookout and let you know if they see any jobs you might be suitable for.

STAFFING AGENCIES

These are dinosaurs that seem to be slowly dying out, but entertainment industry-specific staffing agencies do exist. Just give it a quick Google. However, the jobs will most likely not get you any closer to the writer's room. They are more likely to get you a temp job at a network, studio, management company, or agency. And that's not necessarily a bad thing. Many people make the jump to an actual TV show from these kinds of places. Again, it's all about meeting people.

COLD CALLING/PRODUCTION WEEKLY

This is a truly Hollywood way of getting in that I actually have seen work multiple times: cold calling productions. There are phone numbers for the major studios online, and sometimes you can find your way to the offices of specific shows. There is also a weekly listing of all TV and film productions currently in operation called Production Weekly (productionweekly.com), which charges a subscription for access. It gives you a list of detailed information of every production shooting right now, and often has phone numbers for their production offices. I have multiple friends who have called, somehow made it to the right person, and then asked if they were hiring. The bigger studio productions will be more difficult to navigate, but the smaller production companies will have far fewer roadblocks to reach the person you need to speak with.

SOCIAL MEDIA & REDDIT

I want to present a word of caution with this one. I've never seen somebody get a job by reaching out to a writer or producer through Twitter, Instagram, or TikTok. But there are lively communities of screenwriters on all of these platforms. And Screenwriting Reddit is a treasure trove of industry information. So, although jobs are never posted on social media, being involved with these communities will keep you in the know about the industry in general, and you may even develop a community of people in your position. This is crucial, as you'll find that those who stay and keep at it tend to rise together through the industry.

I'm strictly speaking about finding assistant jobs through these channels. Later in the book, I'll discuss how to use social media to your advantage in your writing career, not just for an assistant job hunt.

This is of course an incomplete list, as each person comes with their own special set of circumstances, opportunities, and resources. So consider this a jumping-off point. Know that these options exist, and then get creative—because you truly never know where your first small break might come from.

CHAPTER 10

JOB POSTING RED FLAGS

Most job postings in this industry have very little information about the job at hand. This is done to protect the privacy of a project a studio is developing, or to hide the identity of a high-profile actor or producer looking for an assistant. There are legitimate reasons to do this. However, it makes it very frustrating for the jobseeker, who can see little more than "Production assistant needed—contact so-and-so with résumé and cover letter."

Every once in a while, however, there's a bit more information in the posting. And though small, there are subtle things to look out for that point to a bad environment and a job that you should *not* pursue.

Look out for any posting that talks about a producer/showrunner/boss with a "strong personality." That is code for "asshole," and they are to be avoided at all costs. Sometimes these types of semi-frank warnings come out in the interview stage, as opposed to the job posting itself. No matter how delicately they put it or how much they're trying to downplay it, I assure you that the reality of the situation is fifty times worse. Another phrase to look out for is when the interviewer or job poster is looking for a candidate with a "thick skin." Nope. Get out.

A more subtle red flag, which I've seen primarily for executive assistants, showrunners' assistants, and writers' assistants is a specific WPM, or Words Per Minute requirement. Some showrunners look for absurdly fast typists clocking in at 100 to 120 WPM. Now, in and of itself, there's nothing wrong with looking for a candidate who can type fast for a job in which the primary duty is typing. The concern is what this represents.

Typically, when a high WPM is sought, it means that a show-runner wants every word taken down verbatim, in meetings or during calls, depending on the position. In writers' rooms, there is a lot of crosstalk, a lot of repeated pitches and jokes; and a good writers' assistant knows when to type and when not to. Likewise for a showrunner's assistant listening in on a notes call. The readability of a document at the end of the day is important; if it's just word diarrhea on a page, that's a lot less helpful for everyone. But maybe this showrunner likes the word-diarrhea way of doing things. And that's fine. However, this type of requirement can be indicative of a very strenuous work environment with people who have very specific ways of doing things. And people in that category can veer into "asshole-ish" territory. Again, this may just be the way the show-runner likes to run things. But in my experience, it is a sign of bad things to come.

CHAPTER 11

MEET PEOPLE AND
BOTHER THEM

Whether you're still looking for your first job or you are years into your career, your goal should always be to maintain and add to your network. Talk to people in the industry and put it out there that you're looking for work. I've been put in touch with countless friends of friends who want to get into the industry. Others have reached out to me through LinkedIn or social media. And I'm generally very happy to talk with them. I get to put on a grizzled voice, pour a scotch, and say "Don't do what I did, kid," before offering some decent, slightly inebriated advice. And after these calls, I stay on the lookout for jobs for these folks. Then I forget about it and stop looking. But then some of them follow up with me, and I start looking again. Which brings me to my point . . . bother people!

It's going to seem unnatural to email somebody who hasn't responded to you in months to check in or ask for something. But it's expected in this industry. There is no clean corporate ladder in which putting your head down and doing a great job will lead to success. The only people who get what they want are the people who *ask* for what they want. So, keep following up with people and keep them aware of what you're looking for.

Make sure to be specific about what you want as well. For example, if you say "I'm just looking for anything, really," it's going to be hard for anybody to bring you to mind when they hear about a writers' assistant position, for example. However, if you say "I really want to be in the writers' room and would like to be a writers' assistant," then somebody like me knows that when they hear about a writers' assistant job, they can contact you. Or maybe they see a Writers' PA job and think of you since it's on the way toward writers' assistant. No matter what comes of it, you won't get any opportunities if you don't put yourself out there and tell everyone what you want.

Two friends of mine were assistants in the writers' office of a very popular TV show. One day, they found themselves talking with the showrunner about the industry. And the showrunner, ever curious, asked what they wanted to do in TV. The two assistants were floored. Why would they be here, taking notes and grabbing coffees, if they didn't want to be TV writers? This seemed so incredibly obvious to them that the question seemed like a joke. But the showrunner was serious. They explained that they wanted to be TV writers—to which the showrunner responded "Oh, well, why don't you just go do that?" Jaws. On the floor.

The people you want to connect with or get a job from do not have the same background that you do. Some of them, like the showrunner in question, did not have to work hard to become a TV writer. For some, because of family connections, Ivy League connections, dumb luck, you name it, jobs get dropped in their lap, and they have no idea what it takes for everyone else to get where they are. All the more reason to never assume that those around you know what you want, and make sure to be specific when you tell them. And always follow up!

Now, a final note about this "following up with people" business. I'm not saying to be a psycho and email the same person once a day or once a week, reminding them that you still exist. Use your common sense and reach out when it seems appropriate. And if you don't hear back, wait a few weeks and try again. What's the worst that can happen? You get banned from Hollywood? Yes, that is probably the worst that can happen. But then you'll have a secondary career writing about your Hollywood experience in a guidebook for up-and-coming TV writers . . .

CHAPTER 12

ASSISTANT JOBS

There are many different assistant jobs out there, and no two are the same—even if they have the same title. But there are certain general duties that remain consistent. We're going to start with assistant jobs at the lower end of the TV production world, and rise to the higher-end assistant jobs, finally ending with an assistant job so fancy that it doesn't even have the word "assistant" in the title. As we rise in job title, we'll also slowly get closer in proximity to the writers' room and eventually wind up in the writers' room, where doughy TV writers come to eat $17 salads and sandwiches.

Traditionally, the following jobs were considered a path toward a writing job. You could go from being a PA or Writers' PA, to a writers' assistant, to a script coordinator, to a writer. And many people still consider this a potential trajectory. I once again want to reiterate: these days, only the lucky few are able to get on a show that has enough episodes to prove yourself to the showrunner and move up, and enough seasons to make it into the writers' room. Therefore, while these jobs will be presented in order of ascending seniority, don't think of them as a path, and don't rely on them to usher you into a staff writing job.

Still, each of these jobs will hold value to the budding TV writer; and at the end of the day, you're increasing your network and meeting people. But be aware, these jobs are a complete waste of time if they don't align with your ultimate goals. So pay attention to the duties, the hours, the networking opportunities, and the ultimate value that you gain from each position.

(Note: The salary information is an approximation as of the time of writing. When indicated, union minimums have been given, though expect these numbers to increase in small increments in subsequent years as the IATSE contract is renegotiated. These figures are purely meant as a guide.)

PRODUCTION ASSISTANT

Average salary: Minimum wage

I've already mentioned production assistants several times in this book, because how could I not? The production assistant is ubiquitous in Hollywood. For many people, it's their first step into the business, and the rung does not get any lower. There are many different types of production assistants. Set PAs work on stage with the actors and director, Production PAs work in the production office, and Night PAs and Writers' PAs work in the writers' office.

The PA position is not glamorous. They run the copies, go to the grocery store, stock the kitchen, pick up lunch and/or coffee, wheel around in golf carts and bring actors and executives to their cars, help out on set, perform lock-up—which is like being a human "Do Not Enter" sign—and the list goes on and on.

Most people start as a Production PA, which stands for Production Production Assistant, which I realize is redundant, but whatever, this industry is lawless. The Production PA works in the production office, which handles the day-to-day logistics of running a TV show. While the writers are in their office demanding food, crazy sets, and wild storylines on small budgets, the production team is made up of those who are figuring out how to actually make it happen. For Production PAs, this can mean the typical duties like picking up lunches or helping out on set, but it can also mean catering to small odds and ends you wouldn't expect.

Things I've been asked to do as a Production PA include:

- Lock-up in New York City on Wall Street at 5 p.m. on a Friday—Try telling a stockbroker they can't get in the subway to go home because we're shooting a show about magic or something.
- Buy Virginia Slims Menthol 120s and Uncrustables Grape flavor for a producer who snacked like a child and smoked like a chimney.
- Drive a giant equipment truck with zero experience.
- Make sure an actor knows there's beer if they want, then offer them a beer again only thirty seconds later because the producer was worried they still didn't have a beer in their hand. They still didn't want the beer . . . It was awkward . . .
- Bring a producer's dog to their weekly grooming appointment at the historic LA bar-themed dog styling studio, Chateau Marmutt.
- Have a beer with some crew guys at 6 a.m. after an all-night shoot so they could pad their timecards.

The Production PA is generally not involved with the writers' room. In smaller productions, there may only be one or two PAs for the entire office, and they do it all, including handling writer-related duties. But on larger productions, the production office is completely separate from the writers' office.

So this is perhaps not the most fruitful job in terms of networking with writers, though it is a good place to make it known what you want to do within entertainment. Look, don't scream at everybody that you're actually an amazing screenwriter and this job is beneath you. (It is, just don't say it.) You should, however, make people aware that you want to write. This will keep it in the minds of your coordinator or UPM (these are two of your many, many bosses) that if a Writers' PA job or writers' assistant job becomes available, you would be a good fit.

Writers' PA/Night PA

You've made it into the writers' office. The Night PA position was where I got my start on a network TV show, eventually moving to Writers' PA. For brevity's sake, I'm lumping these two positions together, because a Night PA will take over for the Writers' PA at the end of their shift if the writers' room is still going. They share many of the same duties, and it's best explained by taking you through a day in the life.

At the start of the day, the Writers' PA will awkwardly step into the writers' room to ask what the writers would like for lunch. I say "awkwardly" not because the PA is doing anything wrong, but because nobody wants to decide where to get food from. After much deliberating, the writers will finally pick a place, the PA will call and find out what the soup options are and bring in copies of the menu to everybody so they can circle what they want, write their name on top, and hand them back to the PA. And even though the PA will call and get the soups every time, a writer will invariably yell after them saying, "Can you find out what the soups are?"

That's far too specific. There's no way that happens on every show. This has happened on every single TV show I've worked on, all with different crews and different writers, including the soup part. I don't know why this lunch system proliferated, but it is like this everywhere. On top of that, I've never understood this propensity toward soup. We're in LA. This is a warm climate. Do they think they're being healthy? But I digress.

After putting in the lunch order, you'll have a couple of hours to chill before going and getting the food. A lot of this job happens all at once and then screeches to a halt. Things need to be done now! Fast! Faster! And then there's nothing to do for hours on end, during which time you can be productive and write, or sit and stare blankly at your computer screen while contemplating your own existence. Some showrunners and production coordinators will want you to constantly look busy, and you'll get a talking-to if somebody passes by and sees you on your phone or fooling around online. If you find yourself in one of these situations, it's good to have some work document or spreadsheet you can pull up, furrow your brow, and maybe run your hands through your hair like you're working really hard on something. Oh, and cover your computer and your desk with post-it notes. If you're doing all this, and you've got reminders and passwords plastered all over your desk, man, do you look busy.

Whatever you choose to do, your next job is going to the lunch spot to grab food. Most of these lunch places around the major studios handle big TV productions all the time, and they know the routine. So, it's usually a quick in-and-out task, picking up two big bags of labeled boxes that you hope are labeled properly with the right orders. Depending on the environment in the writers' room, writers can get insane about their food. When it's busy, they're not seeing their friends or family much, and all they're looking forward to is that hour when they can eat and forget about being stuck in a room all day long. I've seen very serious conversations happen between producers and PAs where, like a work evaluation, they've taken a PA aside and tried to ask them why they aren't getting the right food. It can feel like your job is on the line every time you come back, just hoping there's no side of beans missing.

After lunch, the Writers' PA will clean up the kitchen, which has been ravaged by the writers. This is another consistency across my many shows. Writers will forget to put food away, they'll put garbage in the sink, they'll leave the fridge or freezer door wide open, they'll smudge every surface with peanut butter. I don't know what it is about a writers' kitchen that makes those who use it so gross, but again I've seen it time and time again. It's a thing. It happens.

Now you once again have time to cool off and do your own thing. This can be a dangerous time, because some writers feel they have carte blanche to ask the Writers' PA to do whatever they want, including personal tasks. And when you're not busy, that's when they strike. But this is not part of your job. If they have a personal or executive assistant, this may be *their* job, but it is not *yours*. Maybe what they're asking for is not that big a deal, and in some environments this type of extracurricular task is expected. Still, it's inappropriate, and you should feel free to talk to your production coordinator (your direct supervisor) about it.

Some personal tasks my fellow Writers' PAs and I have been asked to do by writers:

- Buy beer
- Buy Plan B
- Buy a fountain Diet Coke specifically from McDonald's
- Park their car
- Take their car to the car wash
- Heat up their lunch in the microwave
- Flex
- Buy weed
- Buy a butt plug (this was later rescinded when HR concerns were brought up)
- Contact Google to replace the face that always shows up when they Google themselves with their own face
- Chase a bird out of the office
- Use their debit card to take hundreds of dollars out of the ATM which, when returned, I was told to keep as a bonus (aww, it ended nice)

But assuming you are not tasked with nonsense, if you're on a show with a cool showrunner, you may be able to ask to sit in the room during a rewrite or during story breaking. This is a good time to get a taste of the writers' room and see what it's all about.

Around evening time, the Writers' PA duties are passed on to the Night PA, who will be on for the rest of the night and will usually be the last one in the building. Again, on smaller productions, this role may not exist, and all duties will be handled by one PA. But for those on bigger productions, the duties will be segmented. The Night PA's first order of business is getting dinner. Much like earlier with lunch, the Night PA will awkwardly poke their head into the writers' room and ask: "Dinner?" The writers will all look to the showrunner. This is the last hope the writers have of an early night. If the showrunner says no, but there is clearly still a ton of work to be done, the writers will be pissed because they'll be hungry, unfed, and will still get out late. If the showrunner says yes, they'll be pissed because it means they're for sure staying late. The only good answer is "No, we're almost done."

Assuming things in the writers' room are not going well and you do have to get dinner, after grabbing the food the production office is usually winding down and most people are leaving. So it's just you, the writers, the writers' assistant, the script coordinator, and maybe a few editors in some blacked-out editing pods down the way. Essentially, it's pretty empty and pretty open for you to do whatever the hell you want. So work on your writing, watch your Netflix, consider the fact that you have a (insert education level here) degree and spent your day picking up lunch and coffee.

You're free until the script comes out, which for me has happened as early as 3 p.m. and as late as 6 a.m. the next day. Once the script is proofed and sent out by the writers' assistant and script coordinator, you take a copy of the script and start the copying machines. On big studio TV shows, you'll make over a hundred copies for everybody in the writers' office, the production office, and the stage—including the actors. Scripts will also be made for the studio execs, the art department, the wardrobe department, and any other department that works on the lot, and you'll deliver them around the studio.

During these deliveries, you are driving the show's golf cart like a crazy person because it's late, there's nobody around, and it's fun. You might even have music playing and, if you keep your eyes open, maybe you even see some rogue raccoons or cats. The WB studio has a lot of wildlife living on it. The old LA zoo used to be right down the road, and, when they moved the zoo, some of the birds got out and took refuge on the extensive Warner Bros. lot, in addition to the various animals that descend from the foothills every evening. Night PA, beware.

So, you've passed out all the scripts and cleaned up the writer's room. You should be good to go home, right? Well, on some shows, yes. But other shows still haven't acknowledged the invention of email and printers, so you will take the remaining scripts and drive to the actors' houses to deliver them at ungodly hours. This will rack up some mileage, which you'll be reimbursed for, so make sure to keep track of (and then ever so slightly inflate) those mileage numbers.

The Night PA position is a mixed bag. Technically you are the lowest person on the totem pole in the whole office, aside from maybe an intern. However, you do get to be close to the writers. You may also catch the script coordinator or writers' assistant with nothing to do. If you want to get into the room as an assistant, that is the job you want. So, if you can help them out in any way, they may look to you to fill their spot if they move up or leave.

SHOWRUNNER'S ASSISTANT

Average salary: $19-$22/hour

ASSISTANT JOBS   101

This is the only job on the list slightly outside what is traditionally considered the "assistant path" toward becoming a staff writer. (Again, "assistant path" is heavily within quotes because this path is broken.) Some PAs will get bumped up to this role, as it is more senior and comes with more responsibility and higher pay; but in terms of getting yourself closer to the room, this isn't technically the jump you want to make. This job does, however, position you well in terms of getting to know the showrunner.

The showrunner's assistant's job duties really depend on the showrunner. I've seen some instances where SAs had very minimal responsibilities, and others that pretty much ran the writers' office as the de facto supervisor for the PAs. Generally speaking, they manage the showrunner's calendar, answer their phone, and keep them abreast of any meetings they might have. They also control all communication with the showrunner and act as the gatekeeper for anybody who calls in and wants to speak with them.

Some showrunners will need their assistant to manage literally every single thing in their life. I worked on one show where a showrunner writing team had two assistants who managed so many responsibilities in the writers' office and in production that they were made producers on every show the writers created. In another instance, a showrunner needed so much coddling that they had two assistants right outside their door. They would carefully prepare his meals for him and liaise with his wife to coordinate family outings and kids' after-school activities, in addition to their production duties. It was a nightmare job. If you see a job that looks similar to that, run for the Hollywood Hills, and then keep running because you're an assistant and you definitely don't live in that area.

I have never been a showrunner's assistant. However, I was an executive assistant to a showrunner who, at the time, did not have a show. This meant that I was only there if he needed me, which was almost never. While a showrunner's assistant job can be difficult and stressful, there can be whole months or even years of time when you are paid to do nothing. Let me explain . . .

Many showrunners are very highly paid writers who have been around for a long time. Often they are on overall deals with the studio (which I described in the Writers section). So, when their show is in production, they are getting paid through their overall deal, which will cover their salary and their assistant's salary. And when they're not in production, they're still getting paid and so is their assistant.

This can mean months of time when the showrunner will tell their assistant "Don't come into the office, I'm gonna screw off with my family for a few weeks and I'll email you if I need anything." Some generous showrunners go months without talking to their assistants while the checks keep rolling in. Pretty damn good deal. But be warned, there are showrunners that will transition all the assistant's show duties to personal assistant duties. The assistant will have to keep working throughout any hiatus or downtime that others may be enjoying. This should be explained at the start of the job and, if so, that's fine. But clearly one of these showrunner's assistant gigs described above is better than the other.

Lastly, the showrunner's assistant's job is usually not an entry-level position. They tend to look for someone with experience in the industry, either at an agency or a management company, or on another show. And yet, they are not in a union and still suffer similarly low pay and terrible benefits that all production assistants deal with. There is a movement right now for the showrunner's assistants to join the writers' assistants and script coordinators in the IATSE union, but at this moment they still lack protection. Hopefully things will change soon. Can you imagine being a showrunner's assistant to somebody on an overall deal who's in Europe for two months AND you have good insurance and good pay? That is the good life, and I wish that for these folks.

WRITERS' ASSISTANTS AND SCRIPT COORDINATORS

IATSE Union Minimum: $26/hour based on a 40 hour/week guarantee as of the writing of this book. Some are able to negotiate higher rates, or 50- or 60-hour/week guarantees.

Other than showrunning, these are the hardest jobs in a TV writers' office—writers included. And I'm not just saying that because this is where I spent most of my time as an assistant and I'm biased and want my damn credit. They're stressful positions where, if things go wrong, the finger gets pointed squarely at you. But if things go right . . . well, nobody notices anything at all.

These positions are responsible for the script formatting, editing, distribution, research, and note-taking. When the writers collectively make changes to a script in the writers' room, the writers' assistant (WA) and script coordinator (SC) are the ones physically typing the words into the computer.

The writers' assistant and script coordinator are the most showrunner-facing positions of any of the assistants. Therefore, the showrunner's wrath and/or benevolence is directed most heavily toward them. A good showrunner might give the WA and SC a freelance script. This has happened to me, and it truly changed my life financially along with my standing as a writer. With this, your name goes on the "Written by" credits of the show, and you are one step closer to being in the WGA writers' union. Most importantly, you will receive that sweet, sweet script fee money. On WGA shows, this is a gigantic amount of money. Not so much for the already well-paid writers. But for you, it is.

Some showrunners will automatically give writers' assistants and script coordinators scripts every year, regardless of how long they've worked for that person. I received my first freelance script after working at a show for only half a season. Other showrunners will make you wait years before they ever give you a script and consider bumping you up to writer. And still others have a policy of never giving assistants scripts. Don't work for those people. If they don't respect assistants enough to allow them to partake in a nibble of the many riches that come with being a showrunner, you don't want anything to do with them.

This showrunner-facing position has its downsides too. Let's say you don't have a benevolent showrunner. These positions can bear the brunt of the showrunner's inner turmoil. WAs and SCs can be yelled at and belittled and shamed for not being fast enough or for just being "less than" in a room full of "holier than thou" writers. Again, it all depends on the showrunner.

A bit of clarification before we get into the jobs individually . . . On many comedies, the script coordinator and writers' assistant perform almost the same job. The script coordinator is the more senior position and has the last say in a script being ready to be sent out, or distributed (or distro'd, in script coordinator parlance) to the cast and crew. But on most shows I've worked on, the writers' assistant and script coordinator handle all the duties pretty equally.

However, this is not the case on dramas, where there is a much more classic set of duties required of a writers' assistant and a script coordinator, and I will focus here on those duties in the traditional way.

Writers' Assistant

Many folks new to the industry will say that they want to find an entry-level job, like a writers' assistant position. This is not the right thing to say, and it will piss off many a writers' assistant who toiled in PA positions for a long time before moving up to a writers' assistant role. There is a lot to know about how a room works before entering the writers' assistant job. That being said, never hold yourself back if you get the opportunity and you want to do it. Be resourceful and learn on the fly. Plus, you have this book to help you along.

The traditional job for a writers' assistant is to take notes. When writers are mulling over ideas and pitching stories, the writers' assistant is writing everything down. Sometimes, during the note-taking, the writers' assistant's laptop is hooked up to an HDMI cord that is plugged into two big flatscreens at either side of the writers' room, and their document is up so everybody can see what they're writing.

Some showrunners want you to get every word down. They want you to take notes on transitionary conversation between topics, personal stories that lead into a pitch, and you'll end up with a thirty- or forty-page document at the end of the day that you have to somehow make sense of. Lengthy notes sessions are more common in dramas, where there may be multiple complex storylines. In comedies, there's usually just an A-Story, a B-Story, and sometimes a C-Runner.

Learning your A, B, Cs: The A-story is the main storyline in any given episode involving the main character of the show. The B storyline is the second most important story and is given less screen time. C storylines follow in this same pattern but are sometimes so minor that they're downgraded to a "runner," meaning a repeated joke with no story arc.

In most rooms it's fine to get down the gist of what the writer is pitching, and not every single word. In comedies, writers will gravitate to the jokes that are pitched in a room conversation, especially if people laugh. And later they will want to know what those jokes were, almost word for word. Likewise, for important dialogue pitched in a drama, these should be taken down verbatim.

The day will be interspersed with side tangents that allow you a moment to rest, giving your carpal tunnel-addled hands a quick breather. These breaks will often lead to somebody asking you to pull up some information or a funny YouTube clip the writer is trying to think of. Once in a while, this will be something relevant to the story they're discussing. This is rare.

So you've typed for an entire day, you've been listening to constant conversation the entire time, and you have a big ol' vomit document of words. What do you do with it? Some showrunners are fine with you simply slapping the date on the top and sending it out to the writers. But most want a clean, clear document. These notes help a showrunner craft a season and help the writers figure out which areas it might benefit them to concoct pitches for the next day. The pitches that day may not have provided anything clear or fruitful, but the document you send them better look like it did. So, you pick and choose things that writers seemed to have landed on (meaning a general consensus that this is a good story point), and you move those to the top of the document.

At the beginning of the Blue Sky period, the talk will be more abstract and you may be dragging vague ideas to the top of the document. However, as the discussions get more precise and more focused in on crafting the actual episodes, the discussions will be centered on breaking out the exact beats of an episode. During that time, the notes document at the end of the day will have the latest shape the room landed on for that episode at the top, including all the beats throughout, followed by the rest of the important notes related to the story.

On less stringent shows, where not every word is expected to be typed out, it will usually take about an hour after the room breaks to clean up the notes, put the most relevant story points at the top, and email out a ten- to fifteen-page notes document. (Once you get good at it and get a feel for the room, you'll be bolding the important stuff as you type, so that after a quick copy/paste, you can email that sucker out in five minutes and drive home to your heavily roommated apartment.) However, on shows with a word dictator, you could be looking at an extra two to four hours, after the room breaks, of cutting and pasting and filling in blanks and trying to make the document make sense. So, even when the writers get out late from the room and you've been typing literally all day long, settle in. You've got a lot more work ahead of you.

On dramas, there may be a significant amount of research involved as well. The writers' assistant may be asked to verify information or do a little digging into the show bible.

Show Bible: A document that contains the mythology, lore, storylines, and character backgrounds for the series. These are generally created for shows that have been around for many seasons for a quick, easy reference to make sure they're not treading on old story territory. Shows with heavy mythologies, as is prevalent in the sci-fi genre, may create bibles to keep all their backstory and mythology in place. These types of bibles are different from the bibles that are pitched to production companies and studios before a show is bought. Bibles used for pitches are more of a marketing tool to give the potential buyers an idea of what the series will be. For an idea of what this latter group looks like, check out *The Wire*, *True Detective*, and *Stranger Things* bibles, which are all available online.

On comedies, a different beast needs to be tackled by the writers' assistant, and that is being "on screen." This is by far the worst part of the job. In comedies, since there is not much of a delineation between script coordinator and writers' assistant, both jobs go on screen. But in a traditional setting, the script coordinator is not in the room as much or at all. So, I will put this in the writers' assistant section.

Okay, I get it. What the hell does it mean to be "on screen"? The two flatscreen TVs in the writers' room are turned on, the writers' assistant plugs into them with the script pulled up in Final Draft on their computer, and revisions are made to the script live in the room.

A Note on Final Draft: This is *the* screenwriting software used in TV. Across the many TV shows I've worked on, this is the only software that's ever been used. If you're new to screenwriting and don't want to pay the money for Final Draft just yet, I would suggest using any program that can convert files to an FDX (the Final Draft file). WriterDuet has a free version of their program that can do just that.

The writers' assistant will put the script in Revision Mode, meaning that anything that is changed will be written in blue and there will be a star on the side of the page to denote a revision. This is similar to "Track Changes" in a Microsoft Word document and it makes it easier for the actors and crew to scan quickly for changes and make any necessary adjustments.

So, the script goes up on screen and the writers will tell the writers' assistant what to change in the script. Sounds pretty simple and easy, right? It's neither.

Some things screamed at writers' assistants while on screen:

- Faster!
- When I say go up, I mean go down!
- Make it bigger! No, smaller!
- Slow down!

- Up!
- Down!
- Ha, you spelled that wrong! . . . Oh, wait, that's right.

When you're on screen, the whole room is watching every single move you make on the TV and will react accordingly. If you slide the mouse over too much and they think you're going to click on the wrong thing, you might hear an "Ehp, ehp, ehp!" If you're not typing fast enough, you might hear "Faster!" If you're scrolling through the script too erratically, you might hear "Steady!" If you spell something wrong, you will probably be made fun of. (In nicer rooms, this will be followed by a brief semi-sincere discussion about how you have a really hard job. The intentions are good; the results are infantilizing.)

This is where the true nature of your showrunner is on full display, since they're dictating to you all day long, telling you whether to scroll, what to cut out, what to type, when they are just riffing, and when to commit to typing something out. Some showrunners are very good at this dictation and are very nice about it. Then there are the others. Some of the cruelest things I've ever seen happen in a writers' room have happened between showrunner and writers' assistant.

A few showrunners I worked for were yellers. If they didn't like the speed you were working, they would shout. I watched one script coordinator slowly devolve over the few years they spent on screen. At twenty-seven, they had tufts of gray hair and an addiction to Red Bull. Working for these types of showrunners is damaging and creates a terrible environment in the room and in your life. Unfortunately, they are far too prevalent in TV comedies.

On one particular show, the writers' assistant left the room to use the bathroom and came back to be told he was fired. For urinating. How dare he put his need to urinate above the "flow" of revising this episode of terrible television?! Luckily, this showrunner was fired after a slew of other abuses came to light and the main actress declared she wouldn't work if this guy was still the showrunner.

Being fired for going to the bathroom is an extreme example. Well, not an example. It happened. But even with nice writers, you do feel the pressure to stay where you are and keep plugging away. If you step away, all of a sudden there's nobody working on the script and the movement of the room stops completely. Similarly, if someone is in the middle of pitching out a story, it might look odd to just get up and leave the room, even if you're going to do something important. So, it's a bit like you're in middle school and feel like you need permission to use the bathroom.

But there must be good things about this job too, right? Yes. This is your first foray into the writers' room, which means you're finally on the inside, getting to see how TV is made from the ground up. That is huge. It's also a great training ground to make yourself a better writer. It's one thing to study screenplay theory and TV structure; but until you see it in action, it's hard to absorb those lessons into your own writing. After seeing writers analyze countless scripts and countless versions of those scripts, it becomes almost second nature to be able to pinpoint what is wrong with a story or see why people are struggling with a certain line of dialogue, or to understand why the network would never go for certain storylines.

This may also be your first chance to pitch. Some writers' assistants start doing this right out of the gate. I don't recommend that. The writers will likely feel you haven't earned your right to do so yet, and there is a strong chance you will be shunned. From top to bottom, the amount someone speaks is generally dictated by their job title. Now, this rule is very loose. But since you're so far at the bottom of the ladder that you're technically on a different ladder altogether, it's not a great move to be blabbering all the time. A good rule of thumb I've used is to see how much the staff writer (the lowest-level writer) speaks and try to match that.

But in order for anybody to recognize that you might be a good writer, you need to have some pitches that are well received. I've found it helpful to have a conversation with the showrunner and say "Hey, do you mind if I pitch some stuff here and there?" And they're usually cool about it. In fact, most of the time it doesn't even get to that point, because the nice ones will come up to you and tell you "Feel free to pitch if you have anything."

Now, when it comes to pitching, particularly as a writers' assistant, it is best for pitches to be succinct, on topic, and—frankly— very good. As somebody who is not being paid to write or pitch ideas, your pitches have to be better than the average writer in order to get noticed. There's nothing worse than a room stopping dead for a bad pitch or, even worse, a pitch that is not on topic.

Pitching as an assistant is a challenge because you're usually seated in a faraway corner with a computer screen in front of you, and nobody will be paying attention to you. But don't let that stop you. Yell the pitch if you have to. There's no sense in letting an entire season go by without showing your value as a writer. The difficulty increases with the fact that if you are pitching, you are technically doing two jobs at once. The writers get to sit there and muse on their genius, and maybe even write the pitch down so they have it all perfectly lined up before they speak. The writers' assistant, on the other hand, is busy writing down everybody else's ideas or making changes to a script. They have to simultaneously come up with their pitch while taking notes, and then find the appropriate time to pitch it. And as a writers' assistant in comedies, it really helps to pitch jokes. These are always quick, and if they land, they will make the whole room laugh and the credit will be solely on you.

Pitching as an assistant will show you right away if this TV writing business is something you enjoy. If your showrunner expressly does not want you to pitch anything, then you should probably find another show. This job is too hard to waste it working for somebody who only sees you as an assistant.

Script Coordinator

At this point, you've made it all the way up the ranks and your title doesn't even have the word "assistant" in it anymore. Sure, you'll still be looked at and treated like an assistant, but you're as close as possible to being a writer and to possibly getting a freelance script. As mentioned above, in comedies, the script coordinator performs the duties I outlined in the previous section, in addition to a few I will describe in this section. However, in drama, the script coordinator is not in the room. Sometimes they're not even in the office. On these shows, the script coordinator is not getting much face time with the writers and is not able to pitch in the room, which doesn't always allow them a chance to prove themselves in the same way a drama writers' assistant can.

Essentially, script coordinators are in charge of proofreading (proofing, in script coordinator parlance), formatting the script, and handling the distribution of the script. The script coordinator is an expert in Final Draft and will be responsible for denoting changes in each draft and communicating changes to production and to set. When it comes to the script, they are the intermediary between the showrunner and everyone else, and departments will rely on them to get the information they need.

At the beginning of the season, the script coordinator will send out a script template to all the writers to ensure that everybody is working on a document with the same set of formatting rules. This is basically idiot-proofing the script for the writers so they can't turn in anything that looks egregiously wrong. And yet, after coming back from writing a script, some writers will manage to turn in scripts that will make you go "Have you ever seen a script before?" Still, on the whole, you're saving yourself time.

Once the first script comes back from the writer, it's time for proofing. The script coordinator reads through the entire script and fixes spelling, grammatical, and formatting errors. The script is also scanned for inconsistencies and logic bumps that the writer may have missed. And this process is repeated for every new draft, so eventually the SC becomes the person most familiar with every script.

Once it's approved by the showrunner, you'll send the script to the studio and network. Sometimes this is done through email and sometimes through a more secure distribution platform like Scenechronize. Systems like these are used for tightened security and to watermark scripts so they can be tracked in case of a leak. This has become increasingly popular since the Sony hacks.

The Sony Hacks: In 2014, Sony's servers were hacked by a North Korean group as retribution for daring to release *The Interview*, the movie about Kim Jong Un. A ton of embarrassing company emails and information was released to the public. So much strife over a Seth Rogen movie.

The real heavy lifting for the script coordinator begins when preparing for production. This is when a keen eye is particularly necessary. The first step is preparing the script for the table read. This requires proofing just like before, but this time you're putting a script out for the entire production crew, the actors, the executives at the studio and the network or streamer. If there's a misspelled word or a rogue typo or weird formatting, this could trip up some of the actors. A table read gains momentum as it moves forward, and the showrunner hopes the progression and positive energy dissuades execs from giving too many notes. If your missed word or spelling error disrupts that flow, all eyes will be on you. I've seen script coordinators reprimanded for egregious table read-related errors. Before my tenure on one show, an old script draft was distributed instead of the most current one. It happened on a show where there was zero communication from the top, and the script coordinator was doing the best they could. But it nonetheless led to them being fired.

The script coordinator will also be required to create distribution lists for the scripts. This includes everyone on the crew, in the offices, and the executives. It's a rotating list of about 150 people. And there will be emails every day for the first two months from crew members who should be getting the script but aren't, or who have moved on to other shows and don't want to be receiving the script. It's a job in and of itself to manage these lists.

Once a script is ready to be shot, the script coordinator will put out a "shooting draft." This is when the script can get a little wonky. At this point in the rewrite process, you might assume that any necessary script revisions have been made. Wrong. The networks, streamers, and studios have notes on every single draft—and that includes what is supposed to be the final draft, the production draft—and they will continue to give notes and the script will continue to change.

Okay, bear with me, this is about to get a little technical. Once the shooting draft is out, the script coordinator "locks the pages." This means that page count can't change when revisions are made. In Final Draft, once pages are locked, if you add enough to a page, instead of making the entire script longer, an "A page" is created. So, let's say you add some words on page 25 that pushes it over to the next page. Now the page numbers will go 25, 25A, 26. Revised pages are then proofed and sent out to everyone instead of a full script. The reason for this is once the Shooting Draft is distributed, the crew starts physically making notes in their scripts, and the script supervisor (an entirely different position from script coordinator) starts tracking the shots on their script. Releasing "pages" of only the revised parts of the script allows everyone to keep their notes they've made on the rest of the script and insert the new pages without having to redo all their work. Alright, we got through the complicated stuff together. I'm proud of us.

With each new revision, a new color is given to the pages of the script, and those colors are nearly identical across all TV shows. In draft order, it goes like this:

- White (this is the first draft of any script)
- Blue
- Pink
- Yellow
- Green
- Goldenrod
- Buff
- Salmon
- Cherry
- Double White
- Double Blue (and on and on)

If Double White is reached during a production week, something has gone horribly wrong, everyone's script looks like a rainbow, and you are having a bad week. You have my sympathy.

There's a ton of responsibility with this position, and the eyes of the entire production are on you. If you mess up a page that's being sent down to shoot or forget to lock the pages, then you bear the brunt of the mistake and are responsible for slowing down the entire production. And this thought will undoubtedly be in your head every time you press SEND on a new revision of a script, as you pray to the gods of screenwriting minutiae that you didn't miss anything. Because you *will* miss something. Of course you will. There are far too many things for you to keep track of, and the script is constantly changing hands and being noodled with. With a thirty-five- to sixty-five-page script coming out once a day, the chance for error is almost infinite. So, just try to put your head down and triple-check the important things. A misspelled word pales in comparison to an unlocked script or sending out the wrong draft. Or, very embarrassingly, getting the showrunner's name wrong on the title page. That was a weird day.

On dramas, the script coordinator may also be asked to keep the show's bible, which I described previously, up-to-date.

Personally (as if I haven't given my personal take on everything already), I would only suggest taking a script coordinator job if you have vetted the work environment beforehand. I've seen far too many people practically lose their minds from the stress of being a script coordinator. People in this position know more about the ins and outs of the show than literally anyone else and are the only ones—along with the showrunner and line producer—that have the show on their minds at all times. Every time an email comes in, there's a little surge of anxiety, because it might be someone telling them they have hours of work ahead of them and will be ruining their week or weekend. However, unlike the line producer and showrunner, they are not getting rich in the process.

If you do choose to take a script coordinator job, choose your TV show carefully. You don't want your hair falling out or PTSD because there's a new fart joke on page six that you have to distro on Saturday night, and you have to leave your friends to go home and send out new pages for the actors to read. Fart jokes should not dictate your life. If, however, you find the right showrunner and work environment, it can be fine. Stressful, but not abusively so. Just be careful out there. And get those freelance scripts, for god's sake!

CHAPTER 13

THE FINANCIAL REALITIES
OF BEING AN ASSISTANT

Assistant jobs are low-paying and highly inconsistent. You're very lucky if you get on a show that runs for nine months. In a high-cost city like Los Angeles, the measly numbers I included for the various assistant positions allow you to only skate by as long as you don't have any family or other obligations. The cost of living only continues to rise, and the pay levels for most assistants remain stagnant. This leads to a whole host of issues, not the least of which is the fact that it is very difficult for anyone outside of those with family wealth to remain in entry-level jobs long enough to progress. What is meant to be a pipeline into the industry is broken.

The writers' assistant and script coordinator positions unionized fairly recently, which has increased their pay, benefits, and standing. It was a giant boon for an often-ignored and overworked group. After many failed attempts in the past to join the WGA, IATSE stepped up and took them in. However, production assistants and showrunner's assistants have no one looking out for them and have some of the worst pay in the industry. Anybody looking to move to LA and work their way up from production assistant needs to be aware of these realities and the current struggle as studios continue to find ways of cutting back.

For decades, weekly rates were based on a sixty-hour week. Assistants sacrificed low hourly wages for more guaranteed hours, which the studio assumed you were going to be working any-way. However, more recently these supporting roles are seeing the sixty-hour guarantee being reduced to fifty hours—and in some cases, forty—without a compensatory raise in the hourly wage. Studios are also being more stringent in terms of the over-time they allow. I have been on hit shows where overtime hours were thrown around like hotcakes. And I have been on penny-pinching shows where they asked us to fudge our timecards, mov-ing hours to a different day because the studio didn't want to pay for the real hours that the law dictated would be overtime.

I don't mean to discourage you. I only mean to present the real-ity of the situation. You may have to hustle hard in a side gig and/or have a second job, but if you want to do this, you can make it work.

BENEFITS

If you're a PA or showrunner's assistant working for a major studio, you do get health insurance coverage that you have to pay for and is usually contracted out to some other company. (The writers' as-sistants and script coordinators get their insurance through their union, which I'll discuss later.) The health plan is usually . . . just fine. Not great and not terrible.

Unfortunately, as a season winds down and you're looking down the barrel of unemployment, it's important to know that your insurance through the studio will end immediately when your employment ends. There's not a couple of weeks or months you get afterwards to get your new health insurance set up. You are dropped right away. Sure, there's COBRA, but that's generally ludicrously expensive.

UNEMPLOYMENT

I realize it's weird to include a section on unemployment in the same part of the book where I focus on jobs. But I'm doing this for a reason. No matter what type of production you are working on, if you are working for a show and not for someone on an overall deal, you are working freelance. In a best-case scenario, your show will last for nine months. If you are a writer, this job will give you enough money to coast for a while until you find the next job or to bridge the gap between seasons if your show is getting renewed. However, if you are an assistant, this job has given you only enough to get by; it has not allowed you to sock away any money into savings. That's where unemployment comes into play.

Getting on and off unemployment is so pervasive in entertainment that my boss on my first TV show taught me how to do it. Post-pandemic, many more people in the country are familiar with the unemployment system; but each state's system is unique, so it's worth explaining how California unemployment works. You apply on the EDD (Employment Development Department) website by calculating your entire wage for each quarter and inputting the quarterly amount for the last eighteen months. EDD will choose your quarter with the highest wages and calculate your unemployment benefit based on that amount. The range is between $40 and $450 per week. Every two weeks, you will log onto the site and answer questions that will "certify" you for unemployment benefits. Assuming your certification goes through, you will receive two weeks' worth of benefits.

Unemployment is a necessary lifeline in the entertainment industry because, even if you're on a hit show and will definitely be employed next season, you'll still be let go for the hiatus. Unfortunately, we're stuck with a system that forces employees of multi-billion-dollar conglomerates to scrounge for government assistance even when working on hit television shows that are generating millions of dollars in ad or subscriber revenue. So, until studios find it in their corporate hearts to pay their employees better or keep assistants on payroll between seasons, get to know the unemployment system well.

SIDE GIGS & TEMP JOBS

In LA, unemployment, though a nice boost, isn't going to get you very far. So, throughout my time in the assistant game, I held many different jobs outside the industry. I worked with a temp agency that placed me in the HR department at UCLA; and since I made a good impression, they hired me back every time somebody was on leave. This was crucial in helping me bridge the gap between assistant jobs. Other writers work in the service industry, taking jobs as servers or bartenders, jobs that can be flexible with scheduling at the right establishment.

In order to be able to continue pursuing my goal in the streaming era, with shorter seasons and less consistent jobs, I really needed a steady side gig. And I'm finding that most of my colleagues these days need that as well. This is part of what prompted the WGA strike in 2023, the inability of writers to make a living. Well, it's even harder for assistants. I found opportunities in freelance copywriting, advertising my services online and through contacts, and I was able to build some steady clientele that kept me going even while working on TV shows. Other friends have found part-time remote jobs that are flexible enough they can continue their TV writing pursuit and still make enough money to get by.

Keep in mind that this career is not linear. Even if you need to take a job outside the industry, it doesn't mean you're taking a step backwards. That is just the nature of creative industries. So, having a skill or job you know you can fall back on to bridge any gaps helps immensely.

CHAPTER 14

NEGOTIATING YOUR ASSISTANT SALARY

When starting out as a production assistant, particularly on your first job, negotiating your salary will be difficult. Without much experience and with no one to vouch for you, you're likely going to have to take what's being offered. However, as you move along and develop relationships, the situation changes and you should not accept their first offer, even though it will be presented as *the* absolute unchanging salary for your position.

Writers' assistants and script coordinators (and occasionally PAs) are usually brought on by the showrunner or the line producer. In this case, you are in the best position to negotiate your rate. If the people at the head of the show know that you specifically are going to make their life easier, they cannot afford to lose you. Make sure *they* know that *you* know that.

With WAs and SCs, the negotiating can get a little tricky because it's not always clear who you're negotiating with. You will interview and get the job through the showrunner. But everything after that is handed off to the UPM (Unit Production Manager) or line producer. These are folks who did *not* have that amazing interview with you where you explained your worth and got the job. They only know that the studio wants them to pay you rock bottom. If you ask for a rate that's higher than what they're offering, they treat you like you're buying a car. They will tell you they have to check with the studio because "they really said I can't pay over X." Like a salesperson checking with their manager, they will call you back and say "Yeah, the studio really can't do that." But again, maybe you have the showrunner trump card. So you say "Okay, that's too bad. I really want to work with you guys." Sadly, a lot of times it comes down to hardball. And they'll say "Let me see what I can do." And finally, they'll usually come back with "We can't give you that rate, but what if we have a handshake deal where you put X number of hours of overtime on your timecard every week to make up the difference?" Not the best thing, but not the worst thing either.

Sometimes salary negotiations can get funky, and they may offer you a box rental. A box rental is a weird word for the money the studio will pay you if you're using your own equipment at work. They're basically paying to rent your stuff for their production. Box rentals became very popular over the pandemic when employees were forced to use their own computers when working from home. Studios will compensate you for not giving you their equipment to use. But productions will also make up bogus box rentals in order to give you more money that isn't coming through a paycheck. One time, I was given a box rental for fifty bucks a week that said I was renting my office supplies, like staplers and folders, to a major studio. Ridiculous. But hey, I got more money. One thing to be careful of is that some of these box rentals have limits. So they'll say you'll get fifty bucks a week for your laptop *up to $500*. That means after two and a half months, your salary goes down by fifty dollars a week. Don't be afraid to ask for more.

Your hourly wage is particularly important as a script coordinator because you are always on call. Showrunners are supposed to tell you if they need you to be on call during a weekend or during night hours after you've left the office. But the truth is, they don't know when they'll need to change something in a script, or when they'll want to on a whim. And since you're the only one who can get official changes out to the crew and actors, the showrunner may call at any time of any day and ask you to send out newly rewritten pages. For the showrunner, this means tweaking a few words in Final Draft. But for you, this means hours of work. So a small ask over a weekend can ruin an entire day. Many shows will basically ask you to give your whole life to this job, and you need to be compensated accordingly.

Be aware that these jobs are almost always hired last minute. Even at major studios, productions are put together over the course of only a month or two. It's the equivalent of setting up a multi-million-dollar company overnight. And you, the assistant, are going to be the last one to be hired. Even if you interviewed weeks before, and even if you know you're getting the job, you will still not be aware of the start date for a long time. Sometimes they won't even tell you your salary until you're working there already. It's happened to me and many friends of mine. Eventually, I learned not to show up until I knew what I'd be making—and had it in writing. The line producer will assume that you're going to take this job, because "Doesn't everybody want this job?" Everybody will assume this is a learning experience for you on the way to greener pastures, and at the end of the day you won't care what you're making because you're gaining valuable experience and connections. Don't buy into that. This is a job and you're one of the hardest-working members of the team. Get your salary information before you start. You may be dealing with line producers and UPMs who are struggling to put together a show, and your pay is the last thing on their minds. And you'll feel for them. They really are under a lot of pressure. But they are also responsible for doing this and owe it to you to follow state law and tell you what you're going to be paid before you start work.

CHAPTER 15

THE ASSISTANT ATTITUDE
AND WHEN TO QUIT

THE 'TUDE

As an assistant in TV, you're thrust into a room full of many very wealthy people and a few who are not making very much at all. Everybody is there because they love entertainment and desperately want to be there. However, nobody will act like that. Writers in particular will act aloof and put-upon, like this big position that they worked extremely hard to achieve is actually a burden for them. You may also discover that the room is filled with stress and bad vibes. So how are you supposed to behave in this type of environment?

Don't be an "assistant." The "assistant" attitude I'm referring to is the person who acts awkward in front of the higher-ups. They act like everyone else is above them and they're just super happy to be there, and there's far too many "thank you's." This fawning, subservient attitude does two things, both of which will be negative for your workplace dynamic. First, it will make any normal person uncomfortable. People want to relate to each other as people, not as someone who feels beneath them in some way. (If that is the expected attitude in the office, get out now!) Secondly, if bad behavior exists or is bubbling just beneath the surface, this type of attitude will encourage it to boil out of control.

I was a Writers' PA on a TV show with an angry yeller of a boss and an extremely tense writers' room. And the assistants that came before me acted as the writers' personal assistants, which became expected of all assistants that came after. This was a room full of disgruntled writers who needed to be put in their place. When the powers that be turned a blind eye, things got way out of hand.

Now, in no way am I saying that bad behavior on the part of upper-level people on TV shows is the fault of the assistants. Those rooms should not have been allowed to operate in that manner; and that's on the showrunner, the line producer, and the studio. But veering away from that type of fawning behavior will protect you from people taking advantage, and will force people to take you seriously, which is the ultimate goal.

So don't just be the person who's eternally grateful for the opportunity for months on end. Be someone who's ready to do their job and do it well, and then just be your charming self. A showrunner once told me the quality they look for in writers and assistants, which they weigh heavily against all other qualities, is "Do I want to spend eight to fifteen hours a day in a room with this person?" Being a chill, down-to-earth person can compensate for a lot. In my first job as a writers' assistant, I was terrible. I was no good on screen, I was nervous and fidgety when typing in the script, and I didn't understand good episode structure, so my notes were incomprehensible. But people seemed to like me, and I was asked to work on the showrunner's next show, and the one after that.

Years later, when I was much better at the job, but had developed a heavy case of apathy, people liked me even more because they could see that I was doing a pretty good job without trying too hard—and that put everyone at ease. If you have a good attitude and people don't mind being around you, that can make all the difference in terms of your sticking around season over season, or maybe even moving up.

WHEN TO QUIT BEING AN ASSISTANT

Now about that apathy I mentioned earlier . . . I was an assistant for too long. "Too long" could mean something different for everyone. Your first day on the job you might realize this is not a path you want to take, and you'd rather take a more DIY approach. For me, it was the two jobs I took after getting my second writing credit that made me realize I needed to move on.

I was a writers' assistant and a script coordinator on two consecutive TV shows in which I was given a "written by" credit. This got me a few nice paychecks and got me into the WGA. In addition, I was doing really well in the room, pitching a lot of jokes and story ideas that were making their way into scripts. And on each of these shows, I was told by the showrunner that if that show came back for another season, I would be made a staff writer. Both shows were promptly canceled. If nothing else, this should have been my clue that the assistant road was no longer working for me. I had made it to script coordinator, I had been in countless writers' rooms—more than many lower-level writers on these shows—and yet I wasn't getting anywhere. Shows simply weren't lasting long enough for me to make the jump.

However, aside from a few temp jobs up to this point, which paid even less than assistanting, this had been my main source of income. It was also, I felt at the time, the only thing tying me into the business. So I took two more writers' assistant jobs on what turned out to be the most toxic shows I would ever work on. I'd dealt with toxicity before. But what added to it was the fact that I knew I wasn't going to move up. There were far too many people ahead of me. And even if I did get promoted, did I really want to spend any more time here?

It took a pandemic to jostle me awake and force me to realize that I needed to detour, find a different way of making money, and start making my way to the job I wanted based on the connections

I had already made. There was no point in continuing to be an assistant. Those jobs were no longer serving me. In fact, assistant jobs were downright working against me.

I had established myself as a decent writers' assistant and script coordinator, and I was getting referred around town to some pretty big shows . . . as an assistant. It's great when people think of you for a job. It's not great if that job is not what you want to do anymore. In the minds of everyone I had worked for and was reaching out to, I was an assistant, not a writer.

If you decide to be an assistant, make sure to recognize the signs that you should get out of the game and then leave before you get bitter and apathetic as I did. Always be aware that a pivot may be necessary in an industry that's changing as quickly as the TV business. Notice the signs and make your move. Besides, when people ask what you're doing, you can always just tell them you're "in development on a project," which is writer speak for "unemployed."

And as a general rule, if you find yourself in an abusive, toxic environment—including anything that resembles any of the many situations I have outlined so far in this book—don't stick around. Contact HR and your union if you're in one, and then get the hell out of there. No job is worth your sanity or self-worth.

CHAPTER 16

IF YOU CAN, SKIP IT: A FINAL WORD ON ASSISTANTING

If you get offered a writers' assistant job with no industry experience, take it. If you get a chance to be a writer with no assistant experience at all, skip assistanting altogether. There is no rule saying you have to pay your dues. Don't step over people, but don't let anybody in the industry make you think you have to "earn" your position with grunt work. This isn't engineering or brain surgery. This is writing and filming make-believe for an increasingly fickle audience. Keep that in mind as you move along in your career.

Now, in my case, without these assistant jobs, I never would have made the connections I needed to eventually get myself into the writers' room and have a showrunner give me a script. Every industry needs a first step; and for me, these jobs were it.

When I started in the business, I had no idea what any of these job titles meant, and I definitely had no idea what any of their duties were. My hope is that if you choose to take one of these jobs, you go into them armed with the knowledge of what to do, what to take from them, and what to watch out for.

I also wanted to have something that explains what my job was for so many years. Trying to describe to somebody outside the industry what a script coordinator or writers' assistant does is like speaking another language.

"So, you write the script?"

"No, I mean yes, I physically type it."

"So, you're a writer?"

"No, I mean I wrote one of the scripts but I'm not a writer."

"I'm confused."

"Me too."

If you're working in entertainment and want to avoid these endless questions from friends and family, flag this section of the book and give it to the inquisitor. Whether they understand it or not, they will never ask you about it again. Nobody likes homework.

■PART■IV■

BREAKING IN: THE
OTHER ROUTES

Being an assistant is not the only way into the industry. There are routes that can be used in tandem with assistant jobs, and other routes that don't involve assistant work at all. These include studio workshops; screenplay competitions; stand-up, sketch comedy, and improv; or just going out, making something yourself, and putting it out there.

You'll notice that I am not including getting representation in this section, which may seem like a glaring omission at first. However, I'm doing this because it's very rare for somebody just starting out to get an agent or manager. Most reps won't spend any time considering you unless you already have some credits or have made some inroads yourself. And even then, reps will not be your main path to jobs in the industry. They will be a tool just like any other. They may help connect the dots if you have a missing piece in your networking circle and really want to get in touch with a certain higher-up or showrunner. But it will be on you to do the majority of the legwork. Still, it doesn't hurt to pursue representation. Pursue every angle. Just be aware that it's extremely hard to get repped when you're just starting out.

So let's move on to the ways I've seen friends and colleagues get their breaks. Because I made my way into the industry using assistant jobs, I don't have firsthand experience with these other methods, which I'm going to outline in this section. Therefore, I called on some TV writer friends and colleagues and interviewed them to find out a bit more about their experience breaking in with each respective path. Following a description of the path is a "Screenwriter Profile" where you'll get a firsthand account of how each person used this path successfully.

My goal is to make these paths understandable and human. Because, while winning a competition or getting into a major studio's writers' workshop seems like a long shot (because it is), it does happen. Some of these routes may not be appropriate for everyone; others should not be relied upon as the *only* way you're going to try to break in. Regardless, the goal is to allow you to add a couple of tools to your "breaking in" toolbelt, or inspire you to do something completely different and unique.

Let's start with one of the most common ways screenwriters start getting their work out into the world . . . screenwriting competitions.

CHAPTER 17

SCREENWRITING
COMPETITIONS

There are a LOT of screenwriting competitions out there with varying levels of legitimacy. They'll promise huge connections with established professionals, executives, agents, managers, and the like.
And a few actually deliver. Unfortunately, most of the well-vetted,
well-established screenwriting competitions are focused on features, leaving the world of TV screenwriting competitions a bit like
the Wild West.

To make sure that you're submitting your fifty to a hundred
bucks to a worthwhile competition that will genuinely give you a
shot at something more than a certificate if you win, here are some
crucial aspects of the competition to pay attention to:

- **Who is reading your script?** The huge influx of screenplays these competitions receive are handed off to paid
  readers or unpaid interns. Some of these folks have a
  great deal of knowledge of the industry and screenwriting craft. Some of them do not. Therefore, getting past
  the first round of readers in poorly run competitions,
  even with a great script, can be a complete crapshoot.
- **What is the prize?** There will usually be a long list of
  people that the competition will promise to connect you
  with if you win. Google these people. Make sure they

work for legitimate, well-respected companies. Sometimes there will be a cash prize involved and, very rarely,
the mere fact that you won the competition can be a calling card. But that's only the case for a select few competitions.

- **What have past winners gone on to do?** Competitions
  cannot guarantee success, but a pattern is a pattern. If
  you Google past winners and they have never been heard
  from again, that's a bad sign. If many are signed to representation or have sold scripts, or are staffed on TV shows,
  that's a sign that the connections being made from the
  competition are valuable.

Because there are so many screenwriting competitions, I
won't list them all here. The following are a few of the screenwriting competitions known across the industry for choosing
top talent and supporting them to the next stage in their career, either through connections or name recognition. There
are plenty of others not listed that do just that. However, these
consistent mainstays of the screenwriting competition world
will give you a baseline to start exploring, with the first two
comprising the elite category in terms of cachet:

- **Academy Nicholl Fellowship:** This is the Academy's
  screenwriting competition—as in the same people who
  do the Oscars—and it's as big as it gets when it comes to
  competitions. Unfortunately, it is exclusively for feature
  scripts. There is no TV category. However, it is such a
  huge, well-regarded competition that I felt it had to be
  mentioned. (Note: even though this is called a fellowship, it describes itself as a competition, and is different
  from the workshops and fellowships that will be mentioned in the next chapter.)

- **Austin Film Festival Competitions:** Held in nearly as high a regard as the Nicholl Fellowship, they accept features and TV pilots.
- **Slamdance Screenplay Competition:** Slamdance has been around since 1995 and, even if the name recognition isn't quite up to the levels of the previous two competitions, contestants have applauded the prizes and thorough feedback that entrants receive.
- **Tracking Board Launch Pad:** A well-established competition with huge numbers of connections offered to winners. They feature a popular TV pilot competition.
- **PAGE International:** Originally designed as a way to bridge the gap between reps and producers in LA and screenwriters outside of LA, the PAGE International Screenwriting competition has grown in popularity since it began in 2004. They have a long list of success stories and a deep trove of industry producers and executives who they've connected with past winners.

When researching competitions, make sure to read what others are saying about them. Screenwriting Reddit is a fantastic resource for information from winners, rightfully bitter losers, and everyone in between.

SCREENWRITER PROFILE: AARON W. SALA

I met Aaron while we were assistants on a CBS show called *Superior Donuts*. I was riding high after getting my first writing credit as a writers' assistant. Then Aaron came along and put us all to shame by advancing in a screenwriting competition, getting his script in front of producers, and selling it in a newsworthy deal. It's the type of Hollywood story you think can't actually be true, and then boom, the PA turns into a big Hollywood screenwriter overnight.

Aaron's a grounded person, and he's very aware of how unbelievable his story is. As he'll tell you, luck certainly played a part; but when the lucky break came, he was ready for it, due to years of writing scripts and refining his work.

Here's Aaron's screenwriting competition breakthrough story in his own words . . .

GETTING STARTED IN SCREENWRITING

I really wanted to be a director, and I started out making very shitty short films with my friends in junior high and high school. I learned that the only way I'd have something to direct is if I also wrote it. So, I wrote and filmed terrible Tarantino knockoffs and learned over the course of way too long that I'm not Tarantino, and it would just be better if I stopped trying.

Between my sophomore and junior years of college, I was in New York living with my aunt and uncle, and I did some freelance PA work, which led to me being the DP on a web series, which never got released. But I got to work with a bunch of people who wanted to try something and just figure it out on the fly. It was a great learning experience, and it forced me to try to write a feature for the first time. The idea was to write something that I could then direct either when I was home over a break, or while I was still in school if I could cobble together any funding whatsoever without maxing out a credit card.

After the summer, I brought it back and I did a table read with some friends from my film program, and that kickstarted something in me. From that point forward, every trimester I gave myself a challenge to write at least one feature-length script that had nothing to do with a class that I was in. And I came pretty close to that goal. I would do a table read for each one, which was a really great way to figure out what works and what doesn't in terms of dialogue and rhythm, and how stuff on the page translated in person. I found that certain things I loved on the page just didn't work when people actually had to say them, either because they were too wordy, or because it required too much direction or scene description. I didn't write anything that made me go "Oh my god, this is amazing!" But I wrote a bunch of stuff that made me go "Okay, I now know I can never do that again."

ENTERING COMPETITIONS

I started submitting to contests in college as part of the requirements for one of my writing classes. So, I submitted it to The Launch Pad, Stage 32, BlueCat, and a couple of others, and I never really expected anything out of them other than feedback. That was primarily what I was looking for, particularly because they're not cheap. Each competition is around a hundred bucks to enter, and at the time I was a student doing work study, and I didn't have a spare hundred sitting around. So, when considering a competition, a lot of it came down to: "Is this going to be worth it in terms of the feedback I'll get?"

My first feature got decent feedback from BlueCat, and it made it one or two rounds into the competition. Nothing came of it, but I got a little bit of validation to know I'm at least not terrible at this. I submitted to about four competitions in total before eventually realizing they were too expensive to keep doing that, so I would have to pick one or two a year. In total, I submitted four or five scripts before I sent in the one that ended up giving me my breakthrough.

THE BREAKTHROUGH

I made it into the top 10 percent of the Launch Pad Screenwriting Competition, and by the time I found out that I had placed, I was already being put in touch with somebody at Verve, the agency where I ended up signing. What was happening at the time, I learned after the fact, is that once you reach a certain point in the competition, your work goes before industry judges made up of producers, agents, and managers who volunteer to read the scripts. And Verve reached out very fast. I remember getting emails from the competition saying "Hey, we're gonna put you in touch with this person, here's an introduction, here's their email." And I'm clueless. I'm working as a PA on a TV show, and I run over to the EP's assistant to make sure these agencies I'm hearing from are real.

At this point, I'm still in disbelief that it's even gotten this far. And I'm still refusing to believe for a second that a screenplay competition was actually going to get me a breakthrough in the industry. I figured I was going to work my way up for a lot of years to move up to a writers' assistant job, and then a script coordinator job, and then maybe break into a TV writers' room, and then maybe find a manager that also thinks I'm capable of doing features because that's where I wanted to end up. Instead, things fast-forwarded, and I had no idea how to handle it.

So, the script got to Verve and worked its way up the ladder from the guy reading competition scripts, to one of the heads of spec sales. He sent it to a manager at Madhouse, where I'd actually applied to intern when I first moved out to LA. Initially, there was a phone call where they said "This is something we think we can sell, but here's what we think we need to do to get it there." And I'm like "Okay, I'm working a late shift this week, I'll have this to you in a few days."

They then pulled the script from the competition so it couldn't go any further and get any more exposure. In retrospect, that was the first sign that they smelled a sale. Behind the scenes, what happened was one of the higher-up agents at Verve had lunch with a producer who mentioned she was

SCREENWRITING COMPETITIONS

looking for a specific type of movie, and he had just read my script and pitched it to her. Then, apparently, she read it that night or the day after. Meanwhile, I'm at Target in North Hollywood buying Gorilla tape to tape up the leaking moonroof of my Ford Escape because it's the three days of rain in LA and it's turning into *The Shape of Water* in my car. And I get a call that there's an offer on my script.

But both my agents and managers told me not to say yes yet. They told me to do the rewrite they had asked for, and then we'll go back to the producer with the new script that's been rewritten that we think is stronger, and we'll have them ask to make another offer. Does that sound good? And I'm like . . . okay, yeah . . .

And so that's what we did. And then in a week, we had a much more substantial offer put on the table for it and we ended up selling it preemptively, meaning the script would never go wide.

COMPETITION TAKEAWAYS & ADVICE FOR NEWCOMERS

I got very, very lucky. I would not be able, in good conscience, to recommend the route I took to break in to anybody else, because it was sheer dumb luck. I was lucky enough to write a script that the first reader in the competition liked enough to advance. Then I was lucky enough that it got advanced again because I caught another reader on a good day, and then I got stupid lucky that it landed in front of the right person who was judging the competition at an agency, whose boss was somehow having lunch with a producer that was looking for exactly this kind of script the next week. And it was this cascading series of events that makes you go "Are you fucking serious? This does not happen!"

If literally anything about that situation had changed, there is a perfectly good chance that I'm still working as a PA somewhere and writing scripts on the side. And that's not a bad thing. Because at the end of the day, you can't expect success. You have to go in with the mentality of "How do I just keep writing?"

There's no clean way to break in, particularly now for a few reasons. Being in LA is less important than ever before, because everything's on Zoom—and that's both good and bad. It's good because you can do it from anywhere, and it's good because you don't have to drive across LA for a thirty-minute meeting. It's bad because it does make it a lot harder to actually build the relationships that matter. The times that I've sold something after that initial spec sale came from relationships that I had built and established a year before I even came on board the project. And they're both producers that I had either pitched something with before or I had a really good general meeting with and kept in touch. And that wouldn't have been possible over Zoom. It's very hard to maintain those connections when you're talking to your computer instead of a human being.

But no matter what, you have to write. And fail. It's a cliché, but you cannot be afraid to fail. If I hadn't failed so much on my earlier scripts, if I hadn't tried to figure out what I'm not good at by making pale imitations of things that I liked, I never would have gotten to a point where I even thought about writing the script that ended up selling.

If you want to break in, the best thing you can do is write a bunch of stuff, read a bunch of scripts, and watch a shit ton of movies. And teach yourself how to do this. No film program is going to be able to, no matter where you go. You'll gain great connections from school, and that's probably the most important thing, but nobody can just make you a better writer. You have to write and fail and slowly get better.

CHAPTER 18

WORKSHOPS,
FELLOWSHIPS, AND LABS

Because of the lack of pipelines into the industry, years ago, the studios established programs to find and support up-and-coming writers and staff their TV shows. Today most of the major studios and some other industry organizations have variations of the same program, alternatively called workshops, labs, or fellowships. And to incentivize shows to hire participants, at the end of the program, shows typically will pay the soon-to-be staff writer's salary for the entire season. See, TV shows are allocated a certain budget for hiring writers for the writers' room. Writers coming out of workshops are paid directly by the studio instead of it coming out of the TV show's budget. Therefore, a TV show at Warner Bros., for example, could gain a writer without using up any more of their money.

To combat a lack of diversity in TV writers' rooms, many of the major workshops and labs have significantly pivoted their programs toward discovering new and diverse voices. For that reason, most of the workshops presented in this chapter are specifically diversity workshops, labs, or fellowships.

Another pivot during recent years was the movement away from spec scripts as a method of entry into the industry.

TV Spec vs. Feature Spec: Similar term, but two very different meanings. A spec script is one that is written "on spec," or on speculation, meaning the writer is not getting paid to write it. But there is a big difference between a feature spec and a TV spec. TV spec scripts used to be the sample all TV writers needed to have. They are an imagined episode of a TV show that is currently on the air. The writers are not affiliated with that show and are not getting paid. They are writing a sample to prove they can adapt to the voice, style and dialogue of that particular TV show. Back in the day, every writer would have a spec script of shows like *Friends* or *The Sopranos*, and that script would be submitted for potential staffing to any number of shows. A feature spec, on the other hand, is simply an original screenplay. The "spec" part of it in this case just means they are not getting paid to write the script.

These days, executives, showrunners, and reps exclusively want an original TV pilot as a showcase of your writing. However, TV studio workshops are the only holdouts of the old system. For my early years in LA, during the 2010s, I, along with every up-and-coming TV writer I knew, had spec scripts of *Bob's Burgers, Breaking Bad*, or *Veep* that were used exclusively for the TV writing competitions. Today, some competitions only want pilots and some request both a pilot and a spec script as your samples.

Speaking very generally, for most workshops, labs, and fellowships, in addition to submitting writing samples, you'll be asked for a personal statement. If you progress to the next round, there will be an interview with somebody involved with the program. If you're accepted, you'll begin a six- to twelve-month program in which you and your fellow participants develop your scripts and learn from writers, showrunners, and executives. At the end of the program, the studio will arrange meetings with any of their shows that are staffing. So, assuming the interview goes well, the workshop will propel you directly into a staff writer job on a TV show.

However, not all programs have direct routes into a writers' room. Some labs aren't connected to a major studio and have no direct job placement at the conclusion. Nonetheless, these workshops and labs are all hugely helpful for staffing and for your career progression. If you look good, they look good, so they are highly incentivized to help you succeed. In addition, you'll be part of a small but highly connected alumni group who have gone through your program.

It's incredibly hard to get into these programs. There are very few people selected every year, so even if your samples are great, your chances are slim. That being said, most of this career is trying and failing, so you might as well throw everything you can at it and see what sticks.

The following are the major studio workshops, labs, and fellowships, as well as accompanying information about each of them. The application requirements tend to change slightly year over year; and, with studio and network buyouts happening at a fast clip, some of the names of the programs change frequently as well. So, before you start working on an application, check the official website, or look for current information on Screenwriting Reddit.

- **Warner Bros. Discovery Access Writers Program:** A new name for a program with a long history. As of 2023, the WB TV Writers Workshop, which began over forty years ago and was one of the original studio writers' workshops, is now the WB Discovery Access Writers Program. In order to apply, you need two original pilots, two personal statements, a bio, a résumé, and an intro video. If you're selected, participants will work on writing a new TV pilot and will learn about the business and writers' rooms from executives, writers, and producers. The program is one of many within WB Discovery

Access, an entire department dedicated to elevating underrepresented voices. It's worth checking to see if any other programs might suit your career goals.

- **NBC Universal Launch:** Formerly known as NBC's Writers on the Verge, the program has rebranded and focuses on supporting diverse writers. Similar to the WB program, participants receive mentorship from executives at NBC in addition to weekly workshops that help participants refine their work and/or write original pilots. This provides the same type of pipeline as WB, wherein, at the end of the program, the writers are put up for staffing opportunities at NBC Universal Studio's shows. NBC requires two original pilots in addition to a résumé and a personal essay to apply.

- **NBC Universal GTDI (Global Talent Development & Inclusion):** This department contains three diversity programs, two of which are focused on feature screenwriting. However, the Universal Animation Writers Program includes both TV and film writers, focused on programming for ages 3–11. Applying requires an adapted script and one of either an original feature treatment, an original screenplay, a comedy packet, or an original pilot script. In addition, you'll need to submit a résumé and personal essay. This is a one-year full-time program in which participants will be paid a salary for the year. The program intends to develop your project to potentially get it on the air, but there are potential staffing opportunities available on NBC Universal shows at the end of the program.

- **Sesame Workshop Writers' Room:** Run by Sesame Street, the Sesame Workshop is a diversity initiative focused on children's television. Eight applicants are selected, and the program involves mentorship from industry professionals as well as a workshop to create a children's TV pilot. At the end of the workshop, two participants are picked to further develop their ideas. To apply, you'll need a children's television sample (which is generally a short eleven-page script), a résumé, and a personal statement.

- **Nickelodeon Writing Program:** This is a seriously robust workshop. It's a year-long, full-time, paid opportunity. Like the Sesame Workshop, it is focused on creating kids' TV. However, Nickelodeon is geared toward a wider range of ages. In your application they'll ask you to specify whether you're interested in writing Preschool Content (ages 2 to 6), Kids' Content (ages 6 to 11), or Preteen/Young Adult Content (ages 11 to 17). You'll need a spec script, an original pilot script, and a résumé to apply.

- **Fox Entertainment Writers Incubator:** Very similar to the WB and NBC programs, the Fox Entertainment Writers Incubator is a three-month program in which four diverse applicants are selected to work on their samples and meet and learn from industry professionals. At the conclusion of the workshop, Fox promises priority in staffing meetings on the studio's shows. Though they only require one original TV pilot script to enter, they do have a fairly long list of other requirements, including a personal statement, résumé, bio, script synopsis, two additional loglines for different TV show ideas, and two references.

- **Disney Entertainment Television Writing Program:** This program has been around for over thirty years and is similar to the Nickelodeon program in that participants become full-time employees of Disney for one year and are given a salary. They offer mentorship and access to a slew of working professionals and writing program alumni, which includes some real heavy hitters. You will need two original pilots, a personal essay, a résumé, and a "pitch" detailing why you should be considered.

- **Paramount Writers Mentoring Program:** A sixteen-week program in which you meet with studio executives and mentors to help you prepare for a career in TV and to work on your samples. This program is more akin to WB and NBC, rather than the Nickelodeon and Disney full-time paid models. To apply, Paramount requires one original pilot and one spec script, a résumé, and a personal essay.

The aforementioned studio workshops are uniquely positioned to foster your first few years in the industry because of their ability to hire you for one of their shows right out of the program. I've seen many careers get launched in this way. However, there are other workshops and labs that are either not connected to a studio or are more niche within the studios. The following are worth considering:

- **Sundance Institute Episodic Lab:** A six-day program in Utah in which participants' TV scripts are work-shopped with mentors, showrunners, and executives in a simulated writers' room. Though not connected to a major studio, Sundance is such a huge name in the industry that being a program alum could mean major connections and networking opportunities moving forward. The application is quite extensive and includes an original TV pilot, a synopsis, a series overview, a personal statement, a thematic statement, answering a set of creative questions about your project, and a bio.
- **Humanitas New Voices Fellowship:** Founded in 2010, this program is focused on finding unrepresented voices in TV and film and creating mentorship and networking

opportunities.

- **The Black List x WIF Episodic Lab:** The Black List has become an important name in the industry, putting out a list every year of the most talked-about scripts. This has helped elevate many screenwriters and has led to the sale of several feature scripts. On the TV side, The Black List has partnered with WIF (Women In Film) for the Black List x WIF Episodic Lab, a four-week program for female TV screenwriters to learn from mentors and to hone their scripts.

These programs, fellowships, labs, and workshops are some of the most recognizable in the industry. However, there are many more focused on various genre niches and specific cultural groups.

It should also be mentioned that these are incredibly competitive, and it's common for people to apply multiple times. Even though these are workshops, they are still a type of competition, so the best way to approach them is to apply, then forget about it and continue to pursue other avenues.

SCREENWRITER PROFILE: HOWARD JORDAN, JR.

Howard is a talented, funny writer who I met just as he finished the CBS (now Paramount) Writers Program. He became a staff writer on *Superior Donuts* where I was a writers' assistant. Unlike many of the people in the writers' room, Howard was at the beginning of his second career, following a very successful career in advertising.

The following is Howard's take, in his own words, on the tenacity it took to succeed, the risk it took to change industries, the politics at play, and the sizable amount of the job that has nothing to do with writing . . .

THE FIRST CAREER

Ever since I was a little kid, I knew that I wanted to write com-
mercials. When I was twelve, I started ripping ads out of magazines, rewriting them, and mailing them in to companies, not
even knowing that completely separate agencies did the advertising work. My other big passion was sketch comedy on
television. At the time, the big two were *Kids in the Hall* and
Saturday Night Live. But eventually a show that spoke to me
at my core came along, called *In Living Color*.

I knew I wanted to write, and I got to it. In high school and
middle school, I wrote on the newspaper, where I tried writing
my own sketches. And when I got to college, I pursued a degree in marketing, because that's the closest thing I could find
to an advertising program at my school.

After college, I started a graduate program called VCU Ad
Center, now the Brandcenter, which for the last twenty years
has been the best advertising program in the country, but I
was in their second-ever class. I finished school and got recruited by a boutique agency in New York that was very sink-
or-swim. There was a creative department of only seven, and
I was the low man on the totem pole. So, I was twenty-three,
on my own in New York City, all I had was this job, and I said
to myself, "Well, what do you know?" And the answer was
school. That's all I had ever done. So, I went over to NYU and
started taking a sitcom class that was part of their continuing
education program. I was pretty good, and I loved the class,
but still my focus was completely on advertising.

THE SWITCH TO TV

I've now been working in advertising in New York for years,
and I've just been recruited by a new agency and my new paycheck was more money than I'd ever seen. But I knew I was at
the end of my game. I literally had a corner office, looking out

on Broadway and I thought to myself, "I don't even want this. I'm getting the money. I've got the car. I've got the fancy office. And I don't give a fuck." That was my real thought at age thirty-six or thirty-seven. "This is not what I wanna be, how I wanna be, this isn't what I wanna do anymore." But it was all I'd ever dreamed of, so it was a scary moment. I thought to myself, "What do you wanna be doing right now?" And the answer was, I wanted to write TV. But I would be leaving a job that pays $220k a year, I'm approaching forty, and I don't have any connections in TV.

So, I found all my reference materials from the classes I took ten years before at NYU, and I started writing. I came out to LA in the summer of 2013. Until roughly the summer of 2015, I took freelance jobs in advertising, and I made time to write six nights a week—usually from 11:30 p.m. to 1:30 a.m., at a minimum. Every single night after my wife went to bed, I was writing. I entered every screenwriting competition that I heard of, and the first year I got nothing. So, I thought to myself, "What can I do differently?" Around that time, I met a Co-EP on a drama, and I gave her a thirty-five-page script and she gave me three sentences of notes: push all your stories up, your characters all sound the same (they speak in the same rhythmic pattern), and if you're gonna do a spec, then don't get so creative that the supporting characters are the stars of the show. You need the spec to demonstrate that you understand the show. (This was just at the start of the transition from spec samples to pilot samples.)

I take those notes, I rewrite it, and now I'm getting results. Suddenly, I had two scripts in the final twenty-five and one in the final ten of PAGE. I won the Creative World Competition, I was a runner-up for Script Pipeline, and I won the Hollywood Screenplay Contest. Around this time, I met somebody who was a story editor on a hit network comedy, and he said it's cool that you won a couple of contests, but that's not how you're getting in a room. He said, you're Black, you're older (at this point, I'm thirty-nine). You need to look for fellowship programs. You need to research ABC, CBS, Fox, and NBC Writers on the Verge. They only take six or eight people out of one or two thousand applicants, but you need to look into those immediately. So, I did. And I didn't get a single response. I didn't get an interview or anything.

Months later, I was reading *The Hollywood Reporter* and saw an announcement of all the people who had gotten into the Sundance Episodic Story Lab. And it said something like "Margot, the daughter of an Irish cobbler and a one-legged blacksmith, and she's fluent in three Native American dialects and she taught in Africa for four years." And then I read the next one. "Well, James used to be an astronaut and he walked home from space." And I understood that people weren't getting into these programs because of the words on the page, they were getting into the program because of the story they could tell about themselves.

What I say so often now is, write a story that only you can write in a way that only you can write it. I noticed that people had mastered that presentation of self. I've always sold brands; I've never had to sell me.

So I opened up my computer, and I typed . . . "My father was a bookie and a loan shark, my mother was a Baptist preacher. I grew up in a house where faith and vice overlapped every second of every day during my childhood. So of course I'm a comedy writer." My letter of interest may have been eight to ten sentences, max. And in eight sentences, I had three jokes, I was earnest, it was powerful, it was revealing, and it was funny. I also retooled my writing samples, but I know for a fact that that letter of interest changed the game . . . and I got into the CBS program.

WORKSHOPS, FELLOWSHIPS, AND LABS

WHAT WAS LEARNED IN THE FELLOWSHIP

One of the things they tell you when you first get to these fellowships is: "You've got it on the page, but nobody knows who you are. So we're gonna get you an even better sample than what got you in here." And they prepared us for what a writers' room could look like. They told us "You guys all look different, you sound different, you're from different places, and you're gonna be in a room where you might be the only one who looks like you."

They brought in huge showrunners to do mock interviews. They also brought in industry people and active current showrunners to tell us: this is how you move in a room, this is how you pitch, this is how you write on the board, this is why you volunteer to write on the board (because it might be the only time you get to speak). They went over every little nook and cranny of being in a room. I learned that presentation matters, your room image matters. I learned you need to figure out what type of room it is. Is it a competitive environment, a sniping environment, an unhealthy environment? Is there anyone that you can learn from, a mentor?

We also met with lower-level writer alums of the program to ask what a room is like. Then we met with mid-levels, uppers, and showrunners that are all alumni. We call it "cone of silence night," and anything goes. It prepares you, and you realize and accept that only 20 percent of the job is writing—if that.

Toward the end, they told us, "Look, guys, diversity is hard, finding these staff writer spots is hard, and we're gonna help you guys, but all of you need to apply to all the other programs." We had heard stories of people who had done Writers on the Verge *and* ABC, or ABC *and* CBS. You meet a lot of them.

WHAT IT TAKES TO MAKE IT IN THE INDUSTRY

Creative leadership in advertising is less than 5 percent African American. I was in that. For tech, it's less than 2 percent Black. I was in that. If there's a will, there's a way. I knew coming in that if there's a one-in-a-million chance that this can be done, I'm that one. That's the conviction you have to have when you pursue these creative endeavors, because creativity by nature is subjective. And you're always waiting for the next person to approve what you're doing.

And some of the arbiters of whether your great idea succeeds or not have no imagination. That doesn't make you a bad writer. But it does mean you're not getting hired. So, you have to figure out your way. You have to work so that you're always getting better. Don't keep writing the same version of the same script. Always work smarter.

Whatever you have, you've got to work your shit better than anyone else. Whatever you don't have, you have to find the humor in it. It's not enough to just be a good writer. And it's not enough to just be a good salesman. You have to have both, and you have to keep getting better at both.

GETTING INTO THE INDUSTRY TODAY

You need to be writing. When I first got to LA and I told people I wanted to write, they said you need to be over at 3rd and Fairfax (the WGA West building) reading scripts. There's no excuse in an Internet era that you don't go online and find scripts of your favorite shows. That'll passively teach you formatting, timing, craft, and act breaks, just from reading. You need to be reading the types of things you think you want to write. You need to be writing the things you want to be known for, the voice that you want to be known for.

And none of that matters if you're not meeting people. You need to be networking socially. Personally, I'm not a writers' group person; but if you are, make sure to find some like-minded people. And I don't mean that in the political sense, or even on the page. You need like-minded people in the sense that they hustle hard, they're genuine, they have a vision for their future, they will not accept "no." They should be the embodiment of who you want to be. Because in my down moments, I need to be able to look at one of those people and say "Well, they're still at it. And I know they're good." When I was having even an inkling of doubt, in the CBS program, I looked around the room and I felt better. Because I said to myself, "they're excellent. And I'm in here."

I'm not suggesting that anything I've shared with you today is or was or will be easy. But it comes back to asking yourself: "Do you want it or not?"

CHAPTER 19

STAND-UP, IMPROV,
AND SKETCH COMEDY

Stand-up, improv, and sketch are somewhat separate pursuits from episodic comedy writing. I don't want anyone to think that they should pursue a career in stand-up or improv in order to get into TV writing. Pursuing comedy is hard enough as it is, and being a successful stand-up or sketch/improv performer is equally as difficult as making it as a TV writer—if not more so. That being said, there is a tremendous amount of crossover, particularly in the comedy world, and many comedy writers come from the stand-up, improv, and sketch worlds.

Comedy writers' rooms have a host of different needs. They need to figure out interesting stories. They need to craft the voice of the show. They need to develop their characters. And they need to pack the scripts with jokes. And oftentimes, stand-up comedians or people from the improv world are hired onto these shows and find a completely new line of work. Other times, their performance careers and writing careers progress simultaneously.

I worked on two different shows where a stand-up comedian was hired as a punch-up writer just for show nights. This was a multi-cam TV show, which meant they would shoot in front of a live audience one night a week. The punch-up writer would get the script the night before, write a bunch of alts (alternative jokes) to those already on the page, and be ready, along with the other writers, to pitch them to the showrunner if a joke in the script wasn't working. This person was very quick on their feet and could also riff off a million jokes other than the ones they had written down.

So while I wouldn't say "Become a successful stand-up in order to become a writer," there is certainly a path there. And as you'll see in the screenwriter profile below, sometimes connections made in the sketch and improv worlds can prove to be invaluable in kickstarting a TV writing career.

SCREENWRITER PROFILE: HEATHER DEAN

Heather is a fantastic writer who I met while we were both assistants on the CBS multi-cam *Happy Together*. She was a great person to work with, and, as she herself noted, because of her background in improv and sketch comedy, she was immediately at ease in the writers' office and the writers' room. Since then, she's gone on to write for Netflix and, more recently, was a story editor on an animated series.

Here's Heather's story in her own words about the difference between the Chicago and LA improv scenes, how she was able to use her improv world connections to make it into the TV assistant game, and how her skills as a performer helped her excel in the writers' room . . .

GETTING STARTED IN IMPROV

I went to a performing arts high school where I was warned by a lot of my older friends "Don't go into a creative field, because you'll just be a broke server and it's not worth it." And it all ended up being true. So, to hedge my bets, I went to college for education and nonprofit work. And because I still wanted to do improv, I went to school in Chicago, which is the center of the improv scene. So, while I was studying, I was taking improv classes in the evenings.

My first improv class was an immersive, one-week course at Second City. It was a sketch comedy class, so we got a prompt and had to go off for a couple of hours and write it. And by the end of the first day, we performed it. It was all very collaborative and supportive, and everybody was just testing the water, so it wasn't like anybody was trying to "win the class."

Throughout college, I was on different improv teams and took classes at Improv Olympics. Once I graduated, I went to the Second City Conservatory and dove even deeper into improv.

BENEFITS OF IMPROV

I really connected to the collaboration aspect of it. On a good improv team, everyone wants to have a good scene, have a good set, have a good show, all working together—which is a very different attitude than "I am the star of this." Improv is about being supportive and saying "Whatever my teammate puts down, I'm gonna make sure that I support that choice and make them look like a star." And that collaboration has benefited me in the writers' room. I'm a really good cheer-leader in the room, and a lot of that comes from improv.

THE LA TRANSITION

I had been in Chicago for seven or eight years, and I had been on a lot of teams. I had done the whole curriculum at the IO [Improv Olympics], I had graduated from the Second City Conservatory, and I had even done a Second City showcase for up-and-coming talent. But I was rejected from moving on to the next show. They took almost everyone else, and that was a really big ego blow. I started to feel like I was hitting a plateau with the routes in Chicago. At the same time, I knew there was another avenue I could pursue in LA, seeing what opportunities were there, hopefully leveling up to the next playing field.

I had also written a web series right before I left Chicago, thinking maybe I'll film it or do something with it. Really, I thought I just needed to start practicing writing things. But shortly after moving to LA, a friend of mine connected me to this lesbian-focused production company, and they were looking for content. So, I sold it to them. And by "sold," I mean I made like a couple hundred bucks, but I was still amazed I had actually sold something. I acted in it and we had a professional crew, so it was pretty good quality. And that made me feel like I at least have something to bring to the table, something I could speak about to make me not seem like an inexperienced kid.

So, I'm in LA, I've made the web series, but I'm still not sure if I want to pursue acting, improv and sketch, or writing full-time. And I started seeing that sketch and improv was different in LA. In Chicago, it was coming from more of a pure love of the craft and getting that thrill from being on stage. In LA, understandably, it seemed like a lot more of the performers were doing it as a means to become a TV personality or actor. Still lovely people, but most were there trying to get an agent, which is certainly a path that works for a lot of people. But I had the realization that this wasn't what I wanted to do, and I decided I was going to fully pursue writing.

GETTING THE FIRST JOB AND PA'ING

At the time, I was a server, living the life all my high school friends had warned me about. I had no idea how to break into the TV industry. I didn't go to Harvard. I didn't even go to school for TV and film. I had no major connections. But I did have improv and sketch, and I knew a lot of people were making their way in through that. So I auditioned for an improv show performing for kids and families. I got onto the show and, after rehearsal one day, I was talking to another performer, telling them I wanted to work in TV as a writer, but

I wasn't sure how to do that. And he said, "Well, I'm a PA right now on *New Girl*. Is that something you'd be interested in doing?" And I was like, "Ah, yes, absolutely!" And sure enough, a couple of weeks later, *New Girl* needed somebody to fill in for two days, and asked if I was available. So I immediately called in sick to my restaurant job.

My first day, I dove right into the deep end, which was exactly what I needed, because I had never been on a set before. I remember we were printing script pages for different rewrites. And I asked why they were different colors. And they said "These are for the rewrite." And I had no idea what that meant, but I nodded, "Yes, the rewrites, of course, of course, yes. The rewrites in different drafts are in different colors *as we all know because we are all experienced in the industry.*" It was a lot of "fake it till you make it." I was asking the other PA so many questions and just actively trying to learn. And I was making sure that I worked my butt off in those two days. Any time I was sitting down, I asked everyone what else I could do. I tried to be as professional and respectful and polite and hardworking as possible in those two days. And I also tried to meet as many people as I could without being a creep or overstepping any boundaries.

They didn't need anybody to fill in for another month, but then they started to call, and by the end of the season I was filling in once a week. That season ended, but it seemed people were starting to see "Okay, she's very hardworking, she's reliable, anything she needs, she just does without having to be asked." So one of the other assistants I met on *New Girl* went to work on a new pilot called *One Mississippi*. And a few months later, she left, and there was a shifting of the assistants, and I started working there as an Office PA.

From that show, the production coordinators took a job working on *Speechless*, which was on ABC, and they asked if I wanted to be a PA. That became my first full-time PA gig, and it lasted through seasons one and two. One thing just kind of led to the next, and I started to see that with PA work, once you have a good reputation, the work just kind of keeps coming.

BREAKING INTO THE ROOM

I got my first writing gig based on the legwork that I put in being a hardworking PA. I was on *Speechless* for a couple of years, then I left to go to a new show to keep making new connections. And one of the producers from *Speechless*, after their season three ended, became the showrunner for a kids and family show on Netflix. He reached out to me and my writing partner, who had also been on *Speechless* as a script coordinator. They said "Hey, I know you guys are aspiring writers. You're a lot of fun to be around. I know you're hardworking. If you have a sample script, I'd love to read it." We sent it over that night, which was such a nerve-racking moment. This was our shot. And fortunately, we had a good sample already because we had spent a couple of years working on it. We sent it to him, and he liked it and fought for us with the network to give us writers with zero credits a shot. And that was my first staff writing job.

STAYING EMPLOYED AS A WRITER

Even after breaking in, it is still hard. I have a manager, and I get meetings here and there, but a lot of it is still networking. My last job came from a coworker on the Netflix show that I had been a staff writer on. She was a mid-level writer, and her and I had stayed in contact over the pandemic, walking, hanging out, meeting her babies, chilling, being friends. She was getting coffee with a friend of hers who said they needed some writers for this animated show they were working on for their second season. And my friend said "I just worked with two really great staff writers on my last show. I think they'd be a great fit." That's how me and my writing partner got a meeting for the animated show that we just wrapped on. All word of mouth.

ADVICE TO FUTURE WRITERS

Write as much as you can, work on scripts, work on samples, start writing groups with your friends, or anybody that you know that is a writer. I think that that's how you get better— passing around your scripts to your friends. Even Anton and I, we've passed scripts back and forth saying "Hey, read this, give me notes, tell me if it's good, tell me if it's bad." I think a critical thing is being ready and having something that is good when you do finally get that opportunity. You can be great at networking and as hardworking as possible, but if you're not a good writer yet and you haven't worked on your calling card, which is a script, then you're going to miss that opportunity.

I also think getting improv or sketch experience and honing those skills is so useful for a writers' room because it teaches you to be flexible and sharpens your skills to quickly think of an idea or a pitch. Improv and sketch works on those muscles in your brain, and makes you great at collaborating and harnessing the power of the room. It's also a good way to meet like-minded people who might already be working in the industry.

CHAPTER 20

BE CREATIVE, MAKE THINGS, AND USE WHAT YOU'VE GOT

We've all gravitated toward this field because we like to be creative and make things, whether that be writing scripts, or making movies, TV shows, art, or rants. (For some of us it's also because of our desperate need for attention and/or to be liked, but we'll save that for another chapter.) Today, even with a low budget or no budget at all, you can make something and put your stuff out there for the world to see.

Whether or not you have a craft or art that you enjoy besides writing, if you want to pursue TV writing, it's likely that your need to express yourself is strong. And it's important to indulge that need every chance you get. The "putting it out there" part is the second step, the cherry on top. And the TV industry sometimes takes notice.

The industry is obsessed with IP, or Intellectual Property. This is any story or thing that they can option the rights to and turn into a TV or film. There's a wide range of IP—from toys, like Barbie, to articles or podcasts, that have been turned into series like *Super Pumped* about Uber, or *Welcome to Chippendale's*, to books like *Game of Thrones*, to comic books like nearly every single movie for the past decade. In fact, the obsession with IP is so strong, TV writers wanting to sell their own project often remark that they'd be better off writing the book first and then selling it as a TV show. Of course, this is not what I'm advising anybody to do.

However, you're an artist, you like to create. Don't hold that part of yourself back. And if you see that your art, whatever it may be, gives you an "in," take advantage of that. If it doesn't, that's fine too. At least you did what you wanted to do.

I like to write, and I know a lot about breaking into TV writing. I also wanted to get into the publishing world. But even though they both involve writing, there is not a lot of crossover between the two. So I used what I had. I have a lot to say about TV writing that I felt would be helpful for anybody with similar aspirations to mine. And this ended up being just the right level of niche to attract a publisher to buy my book. I have no idea what this will lead to. But I had a lot I wanted to express and information I wanted to give. I indulged that and wrote this book, and now I'm a published author.

SCREENWRITER PROFILE: SEBASTIAN MARTÍNEZ-KADLECIK

I met Sebastian back in 2012 at *2 Broke Girls*, where I was a PA, and he was the accounting assistant in the house next to mine. (Our production and writers' offices were in Warner Village, a part of Warner Bros. that looks like a perfect white-picket-fence suburban street on the exterior, but inside were offices.) Sebastian is an incredibly talented artist and, when I met him, he had published an amazing comic book, called *Penguins vs. Possums*. My writing partner and I loved his work so much that all three of us teamed up for a pitch at Nickelodeon, and his drawings for that pitch packet still blow me away. (And those shows should totally be reconsidered, because they were great, Nickelodeon!)

In the past few years, Sebastian's career completely shifted after another one of his comic books got a lot of positive attention from producers and, eventually, sold! His story is one of tenacity, perseverance, and following your art, wherever it takes you.

GETTING TO LA

I studied acting as an undergrad and in grad school before making the move to LA. When I got out here, I was doing the struggle, like everybody, but there was a lot of talk about making your own stuff. So I joined two theater companies and a sketch comedy troupe, and I found that I was writing a ton, and I was loving it. It was really cool to take a step back and see how other performers were going to interpret it and bring it to life. But I still was focused on acting. So, at the same time, I was performing with this experimental theater company that did site-specific performances, like on a beach or in someone's living room, or in a museum. So, I'm doing this underground exploratory theater, and I had a friend who knew I needed money, and they referred me to Warner Bros. to work as an accounting assistant, so at least I had a little income.

And even though my goal was still acting, I was doing a ton of artwork during this time, trying to get it in galleries, and having it used for set decoration for TV and kind of cobbling together some sort of bohemian artist's life.

WRITING THE FIRST COMIC

While I was at Warner Bros., I was sitting next to a friend who was a production secretary at the time, and we got to talking about our similar interests in comics and movies. It became this sort of third grade sandbox friendship, like "Did we just become best friends?" So I shared some artwork I had done including something called *Penguins vs. Possums,* which was an idea that I had come up with in college, and had created a story around, but it had only existed as that. It had not been a comic book yet. So he and I came up with a web comic and integrated some of the *Penguins vs. Possums* stuff into that.

I had gotten a table at the Long Beach Comic-Con because I really felt like I needed to fuel the artistic part of myself. And I asked my friend if he wanted to share the table, which led to a conversation about making and bringing a comic book. We kicked some ideas around and eventually decided that, of course, the best idea would be to actually turn *Penguins vs. Possums* into a real comic. I grew up going to comic book conventions, and now I'm on the other side of those tables actually selling a book. And people are buying it, people are asking for drawings and sketches, and it was amazing. And I remember going back to my day job at Warner Bros. the next day and my coworkers seeing me and going "You would so much rather be there right now, wouldn't you?" It was such a high, and, unlike most stuff in film and television, it was so immediate. We decided to do a comic book, we made it, we printed it, we took it, and people reacted to it immediately. It was so energizing to realize that I can get these ideas out of my head into something tangible. It lives out in the world, and there's nobody acting as a gatekeeper.

THE PIVOT TO SCREENWRITING

At the time, even though I got a lot of fulfillment out of the comics, I started thinking about screenwriting, but I had no idea where to start. I thought, how can I be a professional writer if I haven't been an assistant or been in a writers' room at all? But my friends who I created *Penguins vs. Possums* with who had experience as assistants in writers' rooms, they were the ones who said, you could have a real career doing that. They said, what we're doing creating this comic book is basically a writers' room. "The three of us are sitting down, we're pitching ideas to each other, we're deciding how to move the story forward, that's how a writers' room works. You should do this." And that was really the moment for me of realizing this is a path I can take. And my whole mindset changed.

I started working on another story idea called *Quince*, about a girl who discovers she has superpowers during her quinceañera. And I thought this would be an amazing movie or television series, but I had no idea how to make that happen. I did know how to make a real, tangible comic book and how to put that into the world. So that's what I did, and it was published by Fanbase Press, who also did *Penguins vs. Possums*. Producers were interested immediately. I told my collaborators, and one of them said "Well, do you want me to just show it to my reps?" I had no idea that she was even working in film and television. I just knew her through this crazy, weird experimental theater company.

So we presented it to her reps, and meanwhile the comic book came out, and producers and production companies started reaching out to me directly. Then we got nominated for awards, and schools and libraries started to notice, and even more people started reaching out, either to me or to Fanbase Press.

SELLING *QUINCE*

Her reps got us a meeting at Disney. I had always been thinking about *Quince* as a TV show at that point, and this Disney exec was the one who said "Well, I'm in features and I would love to do it as a series of features, like with *The Descendants*." Shortly after, that exec moved from Disney over to Netflix and reached out, telling us he actually had more buying power in his new role.

We had another meeting with him, at Netflix this time. And that sparked interest from other companies. So, in addition to Netflix, we started to meet with producers and streamers all over town. That was one of the most magical times for me. This was before the pandemic, so I was able to go there in person. And to drive onto the Warner Bros. lot and not be there for accounting, but because of this thing that I had created in my brain and in my heart, it was incredible. It was still a completely humbling experience, though, because I got to the gate, and they didn't have my name at security, so I had to pull over to the side and wait for them to make some calls to let me in.

This was a dream project for me. It's something that was inspired by my family. I remember writing down, for myself, "Even if nothing happens, don't forget how cool this week was." After that week, we got some offers, and Netflix was the one that seemed right.

THE MENTAL SHIFT

I was so relieved. My son was on the way, and I thought I was going to get some money before he was born. But this is Hollywood, and this was my first project, so I didn't realize it takes forever to get paid. Still, it was life changing—not in the financial sense at the time, but in that, suddenly, this was my career. I still ended up needing to do an art job for comics to make some money in the interim, but I was on the way to making the transition to being a professional writer. This project was meant to be a comic, and then, because that was successful, it transitioned into something else. It felt fluid, it wasn't forced.

And it got me into a ton of rooms. Once the sale happened, it was like "What else you got? What else you got? What else you got?" It gave me a ton of confidence.

SELLING THE SECOND PROJECT

I had another comic book that I was starting to work on, and I thought it would make a great TV show. I soft-pitched it to a production company I met with, and they asked when they could read the script, which I hadn't even started yet. I told them probably around three weeks. And so I sat down and I wrote this pilot over the course of a month. Looking back, I know now they didn't really care about the timeline, but I was new and naïve, so I was like "I have to get this done in time!" I finished it, and another production company approached and was interested, and got a director attached.

So we did some rounds of revisions based on notes, and took out the pitch that I'd created for the show, and I sold it to Netflix. By this time, I had a manager, and she took me aside and said "Really enjoy this moment, because you took out your first two projects and you sold them both. And they were both Latin-centric projects that are notoriously difficult to sell. Cherish this." And I think underneath that was also a sort of warning that it might not always be like this, where you take something out and it sells immediately.

When the offer came, it was my birthday, and I knew the money from *Quince* was coming to an end because the project wasn't moving forward. And I needed to begin hopping from one sinking stone to the next and keep moving. But that sale really made me feel like this was my career, not just a one-off.

GETTING INTO THE INDUSTRY TODAY

I used to hate nonspecific answers to the "How do you break into the industry?" question, whether it be for filmmakers, actors, or writers, to say "Well, everyone finds their own way." My friend was asking me the other day "What happens when people ask you how to get in? What are you gonna tell them, sell a movie, sell your own TV show, and then get staffed on a show?" That's not a viable way for anybody to try, and nobody should try to recreate that path. That just happened to be the way it worked out for me. The industry is just so different right now with all the streamers, and there's different opportunities for different voices.

But I think the best advice I can give with comics or TV or film, or anything, is to just make stuff. It gives you the experience of doing it. It allows that thing to live. And it is something that you can point to that you've done. I'm not even saying make a comic book so that they can turn it into a TV show or a movie or whatever. Just get the experience of doing it. It's the same thing with writing. The more you do it, the more you'll find out what you like and what your voice is. And I don't even mean that in a super-artsy way, just in terms of technically how you like to write, what works for you, what you're good at, what excites you. The more that I write, the more confident I feel in my writing, the more I understand what I'm doing. Because a lot of this job comes down to feeling confident when you walk into a room.

CHAPTER 21

SOCIAL MEDIA & GETTING
YOUR STUFF OUT THERE

In the past, some screenwriters resorted to writing outrageous scripts to get their stuff floating around Hollywood. Even when TV spec scripts were already fading in popularity, a few "stunt" scripts circulated around Hollywood, subsequently gaining a lot of attention for their writers. There was a *Seinfeld* stunt script set on 9/11, and there was even a *Friends* spec where everyone contracts HIV. But these still needed the right people to help circulate them; and, in terms of capitalizing on the splashiness of the scripts, the results varied greatly.

Stunt Script: A script written for the purposes of gaining attention. These are not meant to be produced and are generally not even used for staffing.

These days, you can get your stuff out there all on your own. Of course, you can have your own website, you can submit writing to magazines or contests, but you can also post your own stuff on YouTube, Instagram, or TikTok. I hate myself for even saying this, because it feels like advice somebody's grandfather will give you. "Hey, have you ever considered going viral?" "Why don't you just be an influencer?" These are obviously ridiculous suggestions, and "going viral" should not be your singular focus. However, despite the small chances of being "discovered" in this way, at least you're making what you want to make, you're honing your skills, and you're developing a community, which is the most important thing you can do.

Every time a new social media app becomes big, the industry takes notice and plucks a select few with huge followings and rolls out the red carpet. It happened with Twitter, Instagram, TikTok, and YouTube. And it will continue to happen as more platforms are developed and blasted out to the masses. In 2022, NBC Universal launched an initiative signing well-known TikTokers to development deals in an attempt to turn their popularity on the app into popularity on TV. Will this work? Maybe. Either way, it proved to be a way into the industry for a few folks who may not have had one if they hadn't been on TikTok.

In 2020, I had the idea to write this book. Unfortunately, with no followers, no email list, and no clout, it was going to be impossible for publishers to take me seriously. So I used what I had, which was extensive knowledge about beginning a TV writing career, and I started making videos on TikTok. Now I have a mediocre following and a publishing deal. Not only that, but I've tapped into an entire screenwriting community and am continuously making connections.

SCREENWRITER PROFILE: MICHAEL JAMIN

Anyone who has dabbled in the screenwriting space on social media has likely come across Michael Jamin, a TV writer who, like me, was interested in getting published and turned to social media to gain a following and attract a deal. What Michael found was an entire world of platform-provided possibilities that enabled him to go beyond his singular focus of a book deal.

Over the years, Michael has done it all—multi-cam, single-cam, animated, live-action. He worked his way up in the industry and became a showrunner. So, here's Michael on his experience breaking in, his take on how to break in today, what he looks for in new writers and assistants, and how to use social media to prove that your stuff is good . . .

BREAKING IN

I came out here after college, in the mid-'90s, and I became a PA on a couple of shows, wrote a bunch of specs, studied, took classes, and I was eventually signed by an agent.

At that time, this agent was the one contact in entertainment I had known when I was still in college. I had sent her a script that wasn't very good. I really just wanted to know if the margins were right. Honestly, I knew nothing. She wrote back "This isn't good enough, but get back to me when it is." So I didn't talk to her until several years later when I thought I had a script that was good enough and I sent it to her, and she was like "This is it!"

So she signed me and teamed me up with this guy, Sivert Glarum, and we started writing scripts together. It took a couple of years, but the first script we sold was a freelance script on *Lois & Clark*, which we got because I had worked for the showrunners a couple of years earlier. So, they let us pitch an episode and bought one. And a couple of years after that, we got staffed on *Just Shoot Me*.

WHAT SHOWRUNNERS LOOK FOR IN A WRITER

The script has to grab me, and the story has to start real fast. If it doesn't start by page four or five, I toss it and move on to the next one. Start fast. If it's a comedy, you better hit me over the head with a big joke real fast, and those act break moments have to pop. I don't even care if act three is no good. If acts one and two are good, we can fix act three.

WHAT SHOWRUNNERS LOOK FOR IN AN ASSISTANT

The writers' assistant position in particular is a very hard job. You have to know the program (Final Draft) really well, type fast, and know all the shortcuts. And you have to know when to talk and when not to talk in the room. It's also important to put in the time, I would say at least a year, before you start asking things of the showrunner, like, "Hey, can I get a script?" First, you have to do your job, which is to be a writers' assistant; after that, we can talk. My writing partner and I have given assistants scripts many times, but only after they've put in some time doing the work. These are really hard jobs and it takes a certain skill. I'm certainly not qualified to be a writers' assistant.

GETTING ON SOCIAL MEDIA

I originally got on social media to sell a book that I was writing. In order to get a publishing deal, you need to have a following. So I was like "Okay, how do I build a following?" And I realized it was by sharing as much knowledge as I could. Give, and you'll get. That's been my feeling with social media, and it's been really good for me.

Last summer, I started performing some of my stories in a small theater. So I went online to my followers and asked "Hey, anybody want to come see me?" And I sold out ten shows. Some people even flew to see my shows. I was amazed. I couldn't have done that before I had a following. Nobody knew who I was.

And the platform has helped in unexpected ways. When I have friends that have projects they want to promote, I'll tell them "Let's do a video, let's tell everybody." It makes me look good in their eyes and I'm happy to help them. And I just announced my latest project on social media with two of the stars of my new show. It's not why I got into social media, but if you've got a platform, you might as well use it.

USING SOCIAL MEDIA TO BOOST YOUR CAREER

You should definitely use social media to get your work out there. There are a couple of people I've discovered on there. One in particular is a young woman on TikTok who makes short videos that are clever and funny. Coincidentally, she's also in the Writers Guild, and my partner mentors her. She'll do really well because she's getting her stuff out there.

It's worked for so many other creators. Social media gives you a platform where you can prove to the world how good you are. This is not my idea. Other people have been doing this for a while. There's Sarah Cooper, who started posting these videos of herself lip-syncing to Trump, not just mimicking but adding comedic bits to it, and that blew up, and then she got a deal at Netflix. There's another woman who started posting funny things on Twitter and got discovered and hired by *The Tonight Show with Jimmy Fallon*. It's a platform. Put your work out there, show everyone how talented you are, and good things will come.

BREAKING INTO TV WRITING TODAY

So many people want to start at the top. They won't say "How do I write a good script?" Instead, they'll say "Here's my script, how do I sell it?" Which is crazy to assume that your early scripts can compete at the professional level. But that's what people do. They only want to start at the top. "How do I get my script into Steven Spielberg's lap?" Well, he doesn't need you.

So start at the bottom, and that means teaming up with other people at your level. If you don't want to go to film school—which I understand; it's very expensive—you can still team up with people in film school. Go to their film festivals, compliment the writer or the director. Even if it's not great, you can find something good about it and say "Hey, I'm a fan,

I'd love to work with you on something, on anything." And that becomes your class, that becomes your circle. And then everyone starts slowly rising and opportunities start showing up. And it happens little by little, they don't look like much at first, but that's how you rise up.

Or you can become an assistant on a TV show, which is a little bit harder, but certainly can be done. There's some luck involved. You could have a bad run of five shows and you're out of a job after a few episodes, or you could get on a hit show.

WHAT THE FUTURE LOOKS LIKE FOR TV WRITERS

These days, I think it's easier to break in, but harder to sustain a career. There's a lot more hustling involved. I hear a lot of people, especially when breaking in, complaining about the constant hustling. I want to tell everyone it's also hard for me, and I've been doing it for twenty-seven years. Hollywood doesn't owe any of us a career. So, it's hard all around.

In terms of the industry changing . . . I remember a few years ago, everyone was telling writers "You guys are going to have to pivot." And I remember thinking "Pivot to what? What does that mean?" I had no idea. And so, like everyone else, I just kept my head in the sand. And it turns out that I think what pivoting means is what I'm doing now. Pivoting means me on social media building a following so I can do what I want to do, and not be beholden to anyone else for a job. I can write my own ticket.

PART V

THE SCRIPT

When it comes to establishing a career writing for TV, the actual writing is only one piece of the puzzle. But it is still an important piece. You can't do everything else—network your heart out, get in the right rooms, meet the right people who have the power to give you incredible opportunities—only to have a half-finished script to show people. That won't work. And having the right samples is difficult. It takes years of reading scripts, writing scripts, rewriting them, working on new scripts, and taking bad paths in order to eventually discover the right path and find your voice—all the while, slowly getting better. And so much of that is learned in the process of just doing it.

This book is not a book about screenwriting craft. There are many great books and online resources about how to structure screenplays that delve into the intricacies of episodic story writing. This is a strategy book. Therefore, I'm going to discuss how to strategize your writing and make that another tool in your toolbelt.

As a newcomer, even choosing what type of script you want to write is incredibly daunting. Do you want to write a prestige drama, a procedural, a network sitcom, or a crazy adult animation? Like me, you may be thinking "I like all of those things!" So, how do you choose which genre path to go down? And beyond that, how do you decide which story you want to pursue?

In this section, I'm going to discuss, in very practical terms, what types of samples you need to have, and how to home in on what sort of genre and story you may want to tell. Later, I'll discuss who to show your samples to and how to approach them. Finally, we'll go into the financials of what it means to write a script for TV.

CHAPTER 22

FIRST OF ALL, JUST WRITE

If you've never written anything before, just start writing. Maybe you suffer from procrastination (like most of us) and think "I'm going to start writing right away . . . but first I'll research three-act structure, then film theory, then I'll read *The Writer's Journey,* then I'll analyze my favorite pilot scripts, then I'll buy Final Draft, then I'll take a tutorial, and then, finally, I'll start to write." I'm not knocking any of those steps. Those are all important things to do. But do them while you're writing, making mistakes, suffering from writer's block, hitting dead ends, and thinking your stuff is crap.

You can learn as much as you want about screenwriting craft, but it's not much use if you're not doing it. So much of what you learn about screenwriting comes from actually putting (what's the equivalent of pen to paper?) hand to keyboard and stumbling your way through your screenplay.

It's important to forget about any sense that what you're writing needs to be perfect, or even good enough to show anyone. Because no matter what, your first script probably won't be a home run. In college, a TV screenwriting professor had us write a spec script of *The Larry Sanders Show,* which had been off the air for years. Back in the spec-writing days of TV, only shows that were currently on the air were usable fodder for specs for staffing or getting representation. The teacher was purposefully having us write an unusable spec script specifically because it was our first script and, therefore, it was probably going to be bad and shouldn't be sent out. It was both a preventative measure but also a way to liberate our writing.

Don't operate under the fear that somebody's going to see your script and judge it. Just get down to writing and start getting better right away. If you're using this book to avoid the actual act of writing, put it down and start to write anything. It doesn't matter what. Nobody's going to see it unless you want them to. So let your freak flag fly.

When I first began writing, the idea of finishing a thirty-minute comedy pilot script was daunting. And even when I had written many TV scripts already, the idea of writing a feature script still seemed like climbing an enormous mountain. That is so much space to fill! What has helped me forget the size of the project and just focus on the task at hand is to make the task minuscule. You don't have thirty pages to fill. Right now, you have one. That's all. For today, just write one page. And then you can do anything else. These small tasks are crucial in making the monumental task into digestible, easily accomplished bites. Think about it. If you want to write your first thirty-minute comedy pilot, write one page a day and you're done in a month! Then your first script is out of the way, and you can start making it better—or move on to something else. Still, you'll have accomplished something many fail to do.

As you continue to progress past your first script, you'll want to put more structure in place before starting to write. But if this is your first script, give yourself a small daily goal and stick to it. It really works. Coming from the TV writing world, even with everything I had written, the idea of writing a book was insane to me. So I gave myself a 5,000-word count goal for each day—mind you, some of this was during the pandemic, so those numbers are high purely because I had nothing else to do. And in less than two weeks, I had . . . something. Not something I wanted to show anyone. But I did have something I could work with. And that base is way easier to rewrite than it is to write from scratch.

If you've written a script before and want to get a little more structure in place before diving into the next one, consider revisiting the "Life of an Episode" chapter and start creating a story area and/or outline before moving on to writing a script. If you haven't written a script before, put this book down and write!

CHAPTER 23

YOUR SCRIPT

Let's start with the absolute basics regarding what you need as a sample if you're going to start a TV writing career. And that is *two pilots,* and preferably pilots that are in the same genre.

That seems a little redundant. What about spec scripts? What if I'm into both comedy and drama?

Pilots are the only thing anybody looks at when it comes to a writing sample. Executives, producers, showrunners, and even fellow writers will expect to see a pilot episode of a TV show from you. As I discussed earlier, spec TV scripts—episodes of TV series that already exist and are currently on the air—were the old-fashioned writing samples. The only reason to have a spec script these days is if you're applying to one of the few studio workshops or fellowships that still require one. And they seem to be slowly phasing them out.

So, that means you'll need not one but two pilots. The reason one isn't enough is that if you happen to get your script in front of somebody who's interested, they won't necessarily be interested in developing/producing/making that story. More likely than not, they're interested in you as a writer. You've shown them something that makes them think they should keep an eye on you; but, just to be safe, there's the ever-present follow-up question . . . "What else you got?" If you're stuck with the answer "That's my only sample," they are not going to take you seriously. You've just proven yourself to be far too green for them to invest in.

A little unfair, right? You wrote one great thing; you can probably write another. But this is a hedge-betting industry. And on the
off chance that this first script is a fluke, they're not going to take
a flyer on you. Executives and producers are looking for any reason
to say no—to your material, to you as a writer. And not being "seasoned enough" is a damn good reason.

WHAT EXACTLY IS A PILOT?

A pilot is the first episode of a TV series. In practical terms, it is
season one, episode one of any show you've ever watched. This will
be the case for your yet-to-be-made series as well. The pilot is the
most difficult episode to write in any series. You need to hook the
audience from the very beginning, set up every character, set up the
pilot's story thread, and set up the larger series story arc—all within
the first few pages. Therefore, when somebody reads a well-written
pilot, whether it's showrunners reading for staffing purposes or
managers and agents reading for potential representation, they
all know that you've done something very difficult. It's much easier to write a spec for a TV show that you know well. It's basically
"plug and play" when it comes to characters and story. But a pilot is
a whole world you're making up from scratch, with characters the
reader can become invested in, and a story that keeps them hooked.

THE STRUCTURE

It's very important to stick to your genre's story structure *pretty*
closely. Yes, in screenwriting, rules are meant to be broken. But
you are the new person trying to get in. If you go off and don't
have any real act breaks and don't seem like you have a firm grasp
of where your series can go, the reader may not know that you in
fact do know the structural rules and can abide by them. This is the
only thing they have from which they're able to judge your writing

ability, and you want to show them that you can write something interesting within the framework they are working under. For example, if your goal is to get staffed on a network procedural, a showrunner may be afraid to staff you if your pilot sample has an extended twenty-minute dream sequence and then no real ending, no matter how amazingly David Lynchian your writing may be. They don't know that you are well aware this would not be appropriate for their *CSI* spin-off. So, work within the structure and make it your own.

There is a traditional five-act structure for dramas and three-act structure for comedies. During the classic network days, these act breaks were timed perfectly to match the commercial breaks. The protagonist finally has a night alone with their crush, they open the door to their apartment, and, uh-oh, surprise visit from the parents! End of act one and cut to commercial. However, with streamers and limited series and all the bingeable content, you'll notice a lot of episodes of TV no longer strictly fit into these structures. But you're the new writer coming in and you're not given the benefit of the doubt yet. So "they," the forces that be, will be looking at your script to see if you understand the basics of story.

WHAT ABOUT GENRE?

Remember when I said your two samples should fit into the same genre? This can mean an impossible choice. You're a renaissance person, you want to do everything. Plus some of your favorite shows of all time are *Breaking Bad* or *The Wire*, but you also love *The Office* and *What We Do in the Shadows*. You're not alone. There is a melding of the genres these days, and there are more and more half-hour or even hour-long dramedies than ever. So walls have started to break down, allowing writers to bounce between drama and comedy more freely. I myself worked in comedy for most of my career, wrote on a drama, and then developed a comedy. The bouncing back and forth is real.

But when you're just starting out, you don't have the luxury of having many different samples in your arsenal, and you certainly don't have the credits to back them up. And you're up against a wall of people (executives, reps, showrunners) who don't have time to think about how you might fit into the narrow niche they're trying to fill.

Let's say you get an agent to read your prestige period drama sample, and they like it, and they ask "What else you got?" You send them a wacky comedy. Now this agent doesn't know what to do with you. They might know that somebody is staffing a wacky comedy. But are you the wacky comedy writer, or the prestige drama writer? They can't classify you in a snapshot and, therefore, you don't pop up front-of-mind when they need a writer for *any* project.

So, at least for your first couple of samples, it's best to pick either comedy or drama and stick to it. And this doesn't mean that your samples need to be anything like one another. But if one sample is a network comedy, it's going to make it difficult for you if the next one is a cable or streaming drama. Eventually you'll be able to flex your genre-defying muscles; but to begin with, the busy people you want thinking of you won't give you the opportunity if they can't first classify you.

NETWORK VS. CABLE/STREAMING

You'll notice I included network and cable/streaming as part and parcel of the discussion of genre. There is a big distinction between the sensibilities, tone, and even formatting of each. In essence, you can think of there being four different types of TV: network comedy, cable/streaming comedy, network drama, and cable/streaming drama.

Of course, these days every type of show is being shown everywhere (and what even is cable anymore?), but these distinctions are still important because the powers that be will still classify your writing into these categories. So, the following is the traditional distinction between the two in terms of style and tone, which may give you an idea of the style of script you want to write.

Network comedies and dramas have a much more formulaic pattern to their stories. They're sanitized, they don't curse, and they follow classic structure very closely because they still have commercial breaks to attend to. Comedies tend to have big, broad jokes, and dramas tend to lean into a procedural type of show, like *Law & Order*.

For cable or streaming, the rules are a little less stringent. The violence, language, and subject matter can be far more adult, and can even push some boundaries. For comedies, think about the difference between a show like *Barry* on HBO and a show like *Abbott Elementary* on ABC. For dramas, think about the difference between *Squid Game* on Netflix and *Chicago Fire* on NBC. Both shows in each example fit into the category of TV comedy or TV drama, but they have wildly different sensibilities.

These types of distinctions won't necessarily dictate where your writing will end up (there are both procedurals and broad multicam comedies on streamers), but it will give reps, producers, and execs an idea of where your writing sensibilities lie. And more importantly, these distinctions can help you decide where you see yourself as a future TV writer. One question that comes up in every TV pitch I've done is "Where would this show live?" In other words, what streamer, cable channel, or network could this be on? When starting to write your script, it will be helpful to keep the answer to this question in mind as you develop the tone and feel of your show.

The actual formatting of your script will also look different if you're writing a network or cable/streaming sample. For network, it's important to include the act breaks within your script. This will tell the audience when an act is over and you're planning on going to commercial. For cable or streaming samples, this is not expected. The general act structure should be there in the writing, but it doesn't need to be outlined in the formatting of the script.

When it comes to having a writing sample to get staffed on a specific show, these differences matter a bit less. For example, a more violent, adult drama script could still work as a sample for a network show, and vice versa. So, think of these distinctions in terms of guiding your writing style, tonal preferences, and sensibilities.

COMEDY VS. DRAMA WRITERS' ROOMS

A final word on genre: the types of writers' room environments you're eventually going to be in will vary greatly depending on whether it's a drama or a comedy room. The egos will be different and the job security will be different. A friend who came up in the industry before me said something that was very telling: "All my friends who came up in drama have houses and families. All my friends who came up in comedy are single and unemployed." There is much more turnover in comedy, and it is much harder to get your writing to stand out because so much is dictated by how you perform in the room. This can make for some contentious, anxious rooms. Those certainly exist in dramas, but they're less pervasive.

Drama has also come a bit further in terms of inclusion, diversity, and work atmosphere. Comedy is still attempting to catch up. There is also not usually a "we need to work until the crack of dawn" mentality in drama, so you may have a better chance at having a life outside the room.

WRITE YOUR VOICE

You'll hear it time and time again in the industry: "I just want to hear your voice." "We just want new voices." It's a nice thing to say because it sounds super deep, but what the hell does it actually mean?

Basically, producers, managers, and showrunners want to learn a little about you by reading your script. This could mean any number of things. It could mean that you have a unique writing style and stand out from the bunch because of your use of a certain vernacular. It could mean that this pilot is based on your own story and by reading the character's struggle or triumphs, they are actually reading about yours. In other words, "your voice" consists of the style, content, dialogue, characters, and/or story that make your writing stand out from the pack. It's whatever makes your pilot sample unique enough that it could only have come from you.

And this might not be obvious at first. My writing partner and I had written ten pilots before coming to the conclusion that we seemed to write a specific type of character, a specific type of story, and a specific type of genre. And even then, we don't stick to that exactly (which is maybe hurting us more than it's helping). When it comes to developing your voice, the worst thing is if your screenplay reads like everything else out there. But when you're first starting out, it's common to emulate what you've seen before—so of course you're going to sound like everything else. However, the more you write, the more you come into your own and develop your own sensibilities, style, interesting story turns, and variations on the form itself. That's when your voice really comes into its own. And that's what the industry is looking for. And I promise that's as abstract as this book is going to get.

If you're just starting out writing and don't feel like you have your voice down yet, it may help to write about something you are familiar with or passionate about. Don't stretch too far and get bogged down in research. Write what you know. If that happens to be sports, or your time in high school, or your aspirations for world domination, that'll be much easier than writing about something you don't care about. I've done both, and the scripts that flowed easier and ended up being better samples were the ones dealing with things I cared about or were about people or situations I've personally encountered.

RELEASING YOUR SCRIPT INTO THE WORLD

There are many ways to get your script in front of people. Screenwriting competitions tend to be one of the first ways many new writers receive notes or feedback on their material. If you're in the industry and you have some assistant friends, they're a fantastic resource as well. Most assistants in writers' offices trade scripts with one another and give each other notes. Most of my friends that I look to for notes are people I worked with on various shows in assistant roles. Likewise, friends are always sending me scripts that they would like notes on. Writers' PAs, writers' assistants, and script coordinators have read more scripts than anybody else on earth. Some of the best notes I've ever received have come from these folks.

It also helps to check online for writers' groups that you can join or create one yourself. Basically, take advantage of any way to step outside your bubble with your writing—and gain different perspectives—particularly before you show it to people in the industry who may be able to help you progress.

Maybe you've met a working writer by chance, or you're a PA on a TV show and you're close to the writers' office. Should you print out a copy of your pilot for every writer and leave it on their desks? No, that would be a bad move. Generally, it's best to develop a rapport with the writers over the course of a season. The good writers will know that you too want to do what they're doing and may ask you if you write. It's great to be able to say "Yes, I do. I have a pilot." Or "Yes, I'm working on something right now." Most of the time they will then very naturally ask to read your script or say something like "If you need another pair of eyes on it, I'd be happy to read." That is an ideal situation.

If this doesn't happen naturally, feel free to ask. But again, don't just bombard people on your first day. Wait until you're comfortable around each other and be a normal person about it. After all, this is a favor you're asking of them. Also, you may find after working there for a while that there are specific writers on staff that have a similar sensibility to yours. It's going to be much more helpful having one of them read your script, as opposed to somebody who you tend to disagree with in the room, or whose pitches you don't like, or who you don't like in general.

In any case, having people at your job know that you're a writer—or, even better, a good writer—can only help. Even if you get some notes that you're not sure are right and nothing comes of it, at least now you are known as a writer.

But I'm just starting out and haven't written anything yet. That's fine. Maybe you're still writing your first script, or you have a script you're not too sure about. If you're asked by someone if they can have anything of yours they can read during this time, just say "Yeah, I'm putting the finishing touches on something new that I'd love to show you when I'm done." This will not only allow you to send them your script whenever you want, but it also may light a fire under your ass if you've been procrastinating.

CHAPTER 24

ECONOMICS OF A TV SCRIPT

Getting to write a script for a TV show is a huge deal. It gives you a little bit of clout, it gives you something to write home about, and it gives you a serious payday. This is especially true if you work on a network show. The money is obscene, and you want to get in on some of that.

The rates for network shows are still far higher than for cable and streaming. On high-budget streamers, there is now a subscriber tier that dictates how much you get paid for a script. In other words, streamers with the most subscribers have to pay the most to their writers based on WGA minimums. The pay gets lower for streamers with fewer subscribers.

The rates you can currently make if you are given a "written by" credit on a TV show are damn impressive.

These are the rates as of the implementation of the new WGA contract in 2023 for network primetime (shows like *Young Sheldon* or *Law & Order*):

- 30 minutes or less: $29,823
- 60 minutes or less: $43,862

Basic cable episodic fees are around $10k less give or take. High-budget streaming shows vary between the network and cable levels depending on the platforms' number of subscribers and the budget of the TV show.

So, this means that every time you see a "Written by" credit on an episode of any comedy on ABC, for example, that person made $29,823. Likewise, for an hour-long drama, that writer is $43,862 richer. Keep in mind, this is paid in addition to that writer's weekly or episodic salary. Basically, in one to three weeks of writing, you can make an entire annual salary on top of your already sizable regular salary.

Scripts can also be split between writers. Sometimes it is credited as "Written by X & Y," and sometimes it's a whole complicated calculation: "Story by X, Teleplay by Y." Traditionally, this means that one writer came up with the story and another writer actually wrote it. However, with most episode ideas being generated by the room and the showrunner doling out individual episodes based on seniority, it often just denotes who is getting paid what. Some showrunners will add their name to every "Story by" for every episode of their show. Writers in these rooms make less money and there are fewer chances for assistants to cash in on that sweet freelance script money.

The figures above represent WGA-signatory productions, which encompass most of what you're watching on TV and streaming other than reality or animation. Unfortunately, there are still many shows that are nonunion or low-budget, and their rates don't come close to what writers in the circles mentioned above are making. There is also a weird gray area with animation. Some animated shows are WGA, which is great. Some are in the Animation Guild, and they make far less. So, even within the totality of writers in Hollywood, there are different circles.

Okay, I get the script fees, but don't writers also get paid when their show is on the air? Yes, there are some extra goodies that come along with writing a script that can provide some much-needed cash when you're between jobs, poor and desperate for work, or, as I've taught you to say, when you're "in development on a new project that you're really excited about."

RESIDUALS

Residuals are payments that come from the WGA after your episode is on the air. The money is based on where the show airs, whether it sells internationally, how many times it airs, and whether it's sold into syndication. These days, residuals can be measly, or they can provide some serious income. In fact, residuals were a very common source of income for writers before streamers. However, in upending the TV model, streamers tried to all but eliminate residuals from the equation. That was one huge win for the WGA in the 2023 strike. There is now a formula for calculating residuals from streamers, which will begin to roll out as this book comes out. But no matter the medium, the "supporting you forever" days of residuals, which existed in the '80s and '90s, are pretty much over. Back then, shows could run six seasons and then get sold into syndication and play on TV for years and years. That almost never happens these days.

The biggest residual check you can get is if you're writing for network TV and your episode re-airs. This first rerun will net you half of your original script fee. So, if you made $29k for your network comedy script, the first time the show re-runs, you are paid $14.5k. That means from writing just one script, you've made over forty thousand dollars. Not too shabby for something that may have just been written by the room. I've never received the rerun check. Apparently, my episodes are best viewed no more than once. But the other residuals were still pretty good. For a network comedy, they start at around a few thousand dollars and slowly peter out over the next few months. By the end, you're getting a few dollars and sometimes even cents.

Lots of things contribute to residuals in varying degrees. Any time somebody watches your episode on a flight, when the studio sells the international rights to your show, when somebody rents or buys your episode, and so on, it all gets tallied up, and you get a paycheck.

The paychecks will always arrive the same way: in a light green envelope from the WGA. It creates a Pavlovian serotonin response whenever you see anything that looks remotely green in the mailbox. You start salivating and hoping that "Maybe three years after they canceled that show, they decided to re-air just my episode. That could be, right? Right?!" Nope. Still, a few bucks for a show you haven't worked on in years isn't a bad thing.

If an episode that you write introduces a character (meaning that character is appearing for the first time), you now collect what are called character payments whenever they show up in an episode. So, if your episode introduces a new villain, for example, and they show up in three or four episodes that season, you are making money for every episode they appear in. The character payment amount is a few hundred dollars and pales in comparison to the amounts mentioned previously, but you're still making money for doing nothing.

My first ever freelance script was on CBS's *Superior Donuts*, and my episode introduced a romantic interest that lasted for a three-episode arc. So, for each of the two episodes after mine, my writing partner and I received a residual character payment. There was also a "Female Hipster" character with one line who happened to be brought back again after appearing in our episode. Without even realizing it, we were paid another character payment for that character. There are many similar instances within writers' room lore—mostly from the time of spin-offs—involving lucky folks who wrote episodes that started a character that was spun off into other shows and for which they subsequently collected cash for decades.

PART VI

THE UNIONS

There are two relevant unions for those rising through the ranks of TV writer-dom: IATSE and the WGA. Unions are more important than ever as the arms race for greater amounts of content has led TV studios to look for more ways to cut costs. And that means paying assistants and writers less, particularly when taking into account rapidly rising inflation. The streamers in particular are known for paying their huge stars and A-list writers big money and giving everyone else less than they were making at networks.

Unfortunately, there is no union yet for production assistants and showrunner's assistants. But due to an aggressive effort on the part of writers' assistants, script coordinators, and the nego-tiating committee at IATSE, WAs and SCs are now part of IATSE Local 871. It was a long and hard-fought victory for a much-beleaguered group of assistants. I was a writers' assistant at the time, and joining IATSE literally changed my life. Collectively, we all got a pay raise, health insurance that would see you beyond a production's end date, and somebody to turn to when pro-ducers attempted to lowball you or when abuses came to light.

But you know you've made some serious advances in the industry when you can join the WGA. However, I want to caution you that it takes a writing job on a WGA-signatory show, or a screenplay sale, to get in. Therefore, WGA membership will sort of happen as your career progresses. It's not something you can lobby to get into. That being said, when you are finally allowed to join, there are some things you should know and multiple tiers of membership that I wished I had known about before joining.

This section is shorter than the others, because these are likely not unions you'll be joining from the very beginning of your career. However, it's important to know what these unions are, and what they can do for you as you progress in your career.

CHAPTER 25

IATSE LOCAL 871

The IATSE union is enormous and has a totally unwieldy name—The International Alliance of Theatrical Stage Employees and Allied Crafts of the United States, Its Territories, and Canada. It has 140,000 members across the United States and Canada and represents all kinds of crafts. They cover animation, makeup, grips, lighting, sound, engineers, painters, stagehands—basically almost anything you can think of that happens on a set. But, for the purposes of this book, the part we're concerned with is Local 871, which represents Script Supervisors, Production Coordinators, Accountants, Allied Production Specialists, Script Coordinators, and Writers' Assistants.

Once you reach the writers' assistant level, you are now forced to join the union. This is not a choice. However, the benefits far outweigh the negatives, which are the fees. The initiation fees are substantial, particularly for someone living in Los Angeles off an assistant's salary. The initiation fee is $1,960, and there will be quarterly dues of $163.63 as of the writing of this book.

Nobody wants to add these fees to their general cost of living in LA, but not only did the union bring a pay raise across the board (and it continues to fight for higher salaries, which they are winning for their members), but they brought benefits. And the health benefits are good.

Once you're a part of the union and you clock six hundred hours on any show, you start to get health insurance. If you're working a sixty-hour guaranteed week, you'll reach this in a little over two months. Then you will be enrolled in MPI—Motion Picture Insurance. You'll have a comprehensive insurance plan that is incuded with your dues. So, after the initiation fee, if you consider the dues as paying for only the insurance (which they're not, they're paying for a lot more), you're getting a steal on health insurance. Especially if you're used to paying $250 or more a month for a minimum catastrophic insurance plan that doesn't really cover anything unless you lose a head or something.

Your MPI insurance plan lets you bank hours. As soon as you work over the amount necessary to initially qualify, you start your journey toward the four hundred hours needed to qualify for the next six months. Once that's satisfied, the same applies for the next six months. Therefore, in only a few months of work, you can be covered for the next year even after the completion of your job. This can be a huge deal in an industry rife with periods of unemployment and the associated stress that comes with it. When my job ended in March 2020, I had a little over a year of insurance before I needed to find another plan.

In addition to health insurance, being part of IATSE means you have somebody on your team who knows the labor laws better than you do. If your rights are violated, you can go to them and they will help explain the legalities of the violation and, if necessary, start a grievance with the offending studio.

Personally, this unionization happened at a time when I was really struggling to cover my rent and bills even while working full-time, and the rise in pay and benefits was a huge help. There was also a feeling of unity and collective action that joining the union caused throughout the writers' assistant and script coordinator community, creating a ripple effect of good will.

All of a sudden on the Script Coordinator Google Groups I was a part of, there were spreadsheets circulating where you could add your salary for greater transparency. You could finally see when you were getting screwed and demand higher pay, armed with the knowledge of who was making what. Studios are increasingly being called out and salary issues are being discussed in a way that remained completely under wraps prior to unionization.

CHAPTER 26

WGA

The Writers Guild of America is THE union for screenwriters. When you think of unions, you probably think of some guys at the docks, unloading crates and telling Ice-T that they haven't seen the girl in the picture. The WGA is not that kind of union. The WGA represents TV writers, from staff writers on up to showrunners, as well as feature film screenwriters.

Entry to the WGA operates on a unit-based system. You need twenty-four units within a three-year period to make it in, and those units come from writing on WGA-signatory shows. For example, my first two freelance half-hour scripts gave me twelve units each, the second of which got me into the union.

If you write something for a WGA-signatory production but don't acquire enough units, you'll be asked to join as an Associate Member, which costs $100 and gets you free screeners around the holidays that you can brag to your friends and family about. There's really not much to it.

Once you become a full member, with your twenty-four units, you are asked to pay the initiation fee of $2,500. Considering the large amounts people make for these scripts, that doesn't seem like it's over the top. But as an assistant whose first script paid for their student loans, car payments, and credit card debt, coming up with the initial $2,500 was difficult. And to add to that, you don't get insurance unless you've made around $40,000 from WGA writing jobs in any given year. Which, for somebody starting out, is not easy.

So I was staring down the barrel of this $2,500 fee and thinking no way am I going to give away that script money that I just earned. But after talking to a few writers and industry vets, I decided to do it. If I was going to pursue writing, I would have to join at some point anyway. So I did. And then something amazing happened . . .

THE AGENCY FIGHT

In 2019, the WGA took a stand against the agencies. The WGA board decided they were tired of hearing from their members that what they most wanted changed was the situation with their agents. The issue was complicated. Traditionally, agents represented writers and took ten percent commission on any writing jobs they got or projects they sold. However, over the years, the agencies started to "package" TV and film projects. Packaging means the agency operates as a production company. They are, in effect, producers; and, for a writers' room, they tend to fill these shows with their writer clients. In turn, as producers and "packagers," the agencies receive an undisclosed amount of the backend from the studio. The deals were growing, and the real numbers were hidden behind legalese that even show creators and executive producers didn't have access to. But the biggest problem was that they shifted the agents' priority from their client to the package itself.

In order to incentivize writers to work on packaged shows, they would dangle the fact that they would not have to pay their agent their usual 10 percent commission. In return, the agency would receive untold amounts of money on the backend. So, the agents were in essence double-dealing. Agents were no longer concerned with what might be a good career move for their client or negotiating higher pay for their client. In fact, it might even hurt them if their client got higher pay, because that would take from the money given to them by the studio. Not a beneficial situation for the writer.

So the WGA got together, and every writer in the union fired their agents. It was a huge deal in the entertainment industry, especially in TV where these packaging deals were ubiquitous. And they won. The agencies capitulated and signed the WGA's code of conduct, effectively ending agency packaging.

Okay, but why are you telling us about WGA and agency drama? In the past, agents and managers were the keepers of information. Studios and networks would go through them to do just about everything. They knew what shows were staffing and which studios were looking for what kind of script. And they guarded this information carefully so you would need them in order to have a fruitful career. When the WGA members fired their agents, all of a sudden there was an information disconnect among studios, producers, and writers. Writers could no longer go through their agents to make strategic moves or to connect with a producer or another writer.

The Writers' Hub

Luckily, the WGA recognized this and created a platform on the WGA website for all the scared writers who had just lost their representation. The WGA began posting on a newly created staffing board so members of the WGA could see firsthand who was hiring and what positions they were looking for. It was also possible to submit writing samples through the site to shows that were staffing. Personally, I didn't find the application part of the site hugely effective, since most shows received a huge influx of sample scripts while they were staffing. But chances are, if you've made it into the WGA, unless you're extremely lucky, you've been around a little bit and you've met a lot of people. So, yes, being able to apply to jobs directly is great. But simply having the information regarding who was staffing was far more important. Knowing simple things like what shows are hiring allows you to get on IMDb and look at those shows and then look at other shows those writers have worked on, and cross-reference those folks with your own connections. TV shows hire writers and form a writers' room long before their announcement ever happens in Deadline. So, being in the know helps you get to the front of the line.

Deadline: Deadline.com is one of the most popular entertainment industry news outlets, along with The Hollywood Reporter and Variety.

If nothing else, this shared information eliminated one of the many barriers of entry for emerging writers. This was one of the HUGE positives for lower-level writers like me during this agency fight. Because, in truth, packaging really meant nothing to me. I'd never had an agent, and I'd never been hired on a packaged show. But finally having access to this previously guarded information was crucial.

Unfortunately, the staffing board has fallen off, and almost no shows accept submissions there anymore. The power seems to have shifted back to the agents once the codes of conduct , or the agency agreements to end packaging, were signed. Hopefully, the WGA rectifies this, because as *School House Rock* taught us, "knowledge is power," and the writers' power is slowly being stripped away as they let this important part of the WGA platform languish.

However, agents are not the only players in the game. Managers are important parts of the puzzle for rising writers, and, more often than not, younger writers are able to find managers before getting attention from agents. During the agency fight, the WGA added resources to help writers find managers. This is how I found new management during the pandemic.

Clearly, this is all still a work in progress, but it's a step toward breaking down the stiff barriers to entry that the industry holds dear. Before the WGA had everybody fire their agent, there was nothing close to this. You needed an agent or manager to know anything about what was going on in the business.

And in 2023, the WGA Writers' Strike made it clear that the WGA Board recognized the direction the industry as a whole was headed and was ready to do something about it and fight for their writers. More on that in the next section.

PART VII

A FREELANCE ECONOMY & THE FUTURE OF TV WRITING

The old days of television are on their last legs. In the past, it was easier to fully sustain yourself as a TV writer. You could rise up on a single TV show, making more money year over year while increasing your ability to maintain that position on another show even if your show was canceled. You could enjoy a robust annual salary based on residuals from prior TV shows you'd worked on alone. You could work steadily on one show for nine months out of the year and have a strong possibility of your show coming back so you could return to that job three months later for the next season. There was a path, there was a trajectory, there was advancement.

For those new to the industry, things are much more difficult. It is a different ecosystem today than it once was. I know very few writers—even working writers—who only write. Most have a different skill, like directing, or acting, that they work on in tandem with their writing. Others have a different way of making money altogether.

Like many jobs in the United States, and across the globe, the TV writing industry has become a freelance economy. You are always searching for the next job. You are always having to meet with new people—writers, executives, producers, agents, and managers. And you are consistently having to do more for less. On top of that, writers' rooms are getting shorter. So, that new, lower pay is over and done with well before the end of the nine-month seasons that the generation before us enjoyed.

This is why so many assistants feel stuck. They might staff on a TV show and enjoy a good year as a writer. But finding that next job is so difficult that often they resort to going back to assistant work. Others move on to different work entirely. There's a reason so many sons and daughters of established writers, producers, and actors make it in the industry; there's a reason why so many wealthy folks make it in the industry: they have room to fail. They don't have to worry about searching for a catering gig on Craigslist when their show ends. But for anyone else coming into the industry, that is the uphill battle you'll encounter. And you'll be battling against those already on the top of the hill.

However, all is not lost. The upcoming generation of screenwriters is the most resourceful group of people to ever break into the industry. You have the ability to write, create, film, and make shit happen. You also have access to the lowest-priced tools in history to create cool stuff. You are likely also used to a freelance economy because the TV industry is just indicative of the way the entire country is going. It will be difficult, it will suck at times, and it might be a long slog through assistant jobs, or even in jobs that have nothing to do with the industry. But, coming from someone who knew nobody coming in, I know you can make it happen. It's all a combination of perseverance, luck, and timing, with just a dash of skill thrown in.

Luckily, writers—and, by extension, anyone working in or around the writers' room—have someone on their side. These issues became obvious to the board of the WGA as they neared contract negotiations with the AMPTP, the group of producers and studios, through which rates, terms, and rules are set for the next three years. And the WGA acted . . .

CHAPTER 27

THE 2023 WGA
WRITERS' STRIKE

The numbers don't lie. Writers are working more and making less. The WGA found, when analyzing writer pay, that, when adjusted for inflation, writers' median weekly salaries plummeted by 23 percent between 2013 and 2023. The residuals I mentioned that used to keep writers afloat between gigs had all but disappeared on streaming shows.

Writers' rooms are smaller, mini-rooms have taken over, and a whole generation of writers (in fact, everyone who is not yet a showrunner) was being excluded from the TV-making process by corporate entities who didn't want to pay more than one person to oversee a show from writing to post-production. This effectively prevented everyone from learning the ropes, all but making it impossible for newer writers, including the recent influx of diverse writers that the industry so desperately needs, from advancing.

On top of that, producers and studios made it all too clear that they intended to fully take advantage of the recent advent of AI and try to squeeze writers out of the writing process completely. (Let me give you a moment to let that settle in.) AI is an information scraping/regurgitating tool, and it's very good at that. Their intention was to scrape past writers' work, for free, in order to make new screenplays, for free.

With all this in mind, the WGA went to the negotiating table, which they do every three years, to negotiate a new contract with the AMPTP. Despite corporate mergers and the incredible arms race for more streaming content in the past few years, the companies still claimed they were broke. The AMPTP claimed losses over the past year, and that it's just not a good time to give writers a livable career.

The AMPTP's final offer during their original negotiation contained only small bumps when it came to minimum salaries and residuals, not even approaching what would make this career livable, nothing in the way of offering writers' room security, a main lifeline for TV writer careers; and when it came to AI, they offered to hold a meeting with the WGA once a year to discuss things . . . basically nothing.

So, at 12:01 a.m. on May 2, 2023, the old contract expired and the strike began.

With our blue union shirts and funny picket signs (a personal favorite of mine that I saw, "Lisa Needs Braces," for the true *Simpsons* fans out there), the writers started marching in front of the studios. Morning and afternoon, writers walked in front of Paramount, Disney, Amazon, Warner Bros., Sony, Netflix, Universal, and others in LA, and many more productions in New York, while cars drove by honking in support of the fight.

The support was intense and immediate, because this fight is not just happening to writers, it's happening to assistants, and it's happening to workers all over the country. They are being asked to do more for less, with less job security and fewer safety nets.

Two days into the strike, a WGA rally was held, during which members from nearly every entertainment union came out to support the WGA. Everyone was feeling the effects of this belt tightening. Impassioned speeches were made from all union leaders, a highlight being Lindsay Dougherty, the president of Teamsters Local 399, who, fully equipped with a Jimmy Hoffa tattoo on her arm, shouted, cursed, and got the crowd on their feet. All the union leaders expressed unprecedented solidarity. They would support the WGA, and they would not cross picket lines.

And productions ground to a halt. As opposed to prior strikes, which happened in 2007–2008, 1988, 1985, 1981, 1973, 1960, and 1952 (that's right, the WGA strikes a lot, and I'm proud of it), the release of new episodes of TV did not stop immediately. Because of streaming and the change from week-to-week production schedules of the old model, many streamers and cable channels had shows banked, and they were able to release them during the strike. Therefore, the immediate effects of the strike weighed far more heavily on broadcast networks than streamers, causing what seemed to be a mix of priorities within the AMPTP.

The WGA has struck nearly every time a new platform has been introduced. There was a strike for cable television residuals in 1981, VHS residuals in 1985, and "new media" in 2007–2008. This was the next iteration. Though what was considered "new media" is now streaming, the landscape has once again changed from a small amount of Video on Demand sales to nearly all of TV.

The other neighboring unions who also negotiate their contracts with the AMPTP—the DGA (the directors) and SAG-AFTRA (the actors)—were next up to negotiate. The DGA, knowing full well that the WGA was likely going to strike, decided to hold their negotiations after the WGA's and used the strike as leverage. They agreed on a contract and signed the world's first union contract that contains stipulations for AI.

Next up was SAG-AFTRA, and the president of the union, Fran Drescher, began negotiating with the AMPTP. A majority of the WGA's leverage, in addition to the leverage of the entire artistic community, was riding on what kind of deal they made.

Now, if you had told me when I left college that a situation involving unions, millionaire CEOs, writers, AI robots, and *The Nanny* was going to come to a head and affect the outcome of my career in 2023, I would have avoided eye contact and tried to make my exit. But that's where we found ourselves.

SAG-AFTRA found they were being stonewalled by the AMPTP, who were unwilling to negotiate on crucial points, among them a change in the model for residuals based on the changed business model for streaming, and, of course, on AI protections. (The AMPTP wanted to be able to film background actors and be able to reuse them in perpetuity for no money.) So, SAG-AFTRA struck and joined the WGA on the picket lines, the first joint strike since 1960.

The WGA strike lasted 148 days, only 5 days shy of the one in 1988, which is still the longest WGA strike in history. Writers stopped picketing, the WGA board voted, and eventually the membership did as well, and they ratified a new contract with the AMPTP. When all the dust had settled, it was clear the WGA had won big.

There was an increase in weekly rates across the board. There is now a viewership-based residual model for streamers, meaning writers will finally get compensation based on how well their show actually does. This was a major first step in knocking down the wall streamers had built around their streaming numbers, which they held on to and kept secret from even some shows' creators. There are higher rates and greater protections for writers in mini-rooms, who had been subjected to smaller pay and shorter employment. There is now a mandatory minimum number of writers in writers' rooms, a major step toward protecting career mobility and longevity. The studios can no longer insist that a showrunner take it all on themselves or winnow out the writers completely towards the end of a season. The minimum staffing numbers are not huge, but they are a starting point, as these protections did not exist at all before the strike.

Finally, the AI component. This contract ensures that Terminators won't be sitting down to write screenplays. The contract stipulates AI can't write or rewrite any literary material, and AI-produced writing can't be used as source material. The writers will remain writers.

There's give and take in every negotiation, and you can't expect to win everything. But the WGA came pretty damn close. This was an overwhelming victory and will protect you, the up-and-coming writer, for years to come. Or at least until the studios find another loophole. Then we'll see you out on the picket lines. Regardless of what fights the future holds, or how the benefits and repercussions of this contract play out over the next few years, TV writing will flourish as a career. Will it be the same it is now? No. Will it go back to how it was? No. A new normal will evolve, and I'm on the side of establishing a better path for the young folks coming in. Use what you know, use what you've learned, and carve out your path forward.

CHAPTER 28

CARVING OUT YOUR
UNIQUE PATH

The screenwriting profession isn't for those that simply want to make a TV show. Sure, that's the end goal. But you need to make sure that you love to write. Because, at the end of the day, it's not very likely you'll ever see what you wrote on the screen. There are scores of successful screenwriters that sell pilots or movies and never see their words, or their version of the story, in the end product. Things are rewritten, changed entirely, or never make it far enough for a sold script to make it into production.

Your ultimate goal should be to write something that everybody sees. But if your enjoyment comes only from the end product and not the actual doing—the writing, revising, passing to friends, adjusting based on notes, creating interesting characters and dialogue—then you are pursuing the wrong path.

And that's fine! There are plenty of other careers in the industry—or outside the industry—that would be suitable for you. Maybe being a producer is a more agreeable path for your interests. Or a creative executive role could offer the type of creative collaboration you enjoy. Maybe you're more interested in the business side of the entertainment industry, and an agency route is more your speed.

On average, 45 percent of WGA members are unemployed at any given time. That's only a little more than half of membership that's working. And that's only among a group that has made big enough strides in screenwriting to even make it into the union.

It's this level of uncertainty and mind-numbing persistence that you need to be prepared for if you want to be a screenwriter. If that way of life is not for you, then it's best to know that now. When I felt stuck as an assistant, I spent many days asking myself why I was doing this. I thought about changing industries, as a lot of my friends had done. And, honestly, a lot of them were happier for it.

Changing Industries vs. Quitting: "Quitting" is a bullshit term reserved only for use in artistic fields. The "failure" it presumes makes creatives fearful of making change and causes many to legitimize putting up with terrible conditions for far too long. Think of any other industry—doctors, lawyers, engineers. If they switch gears and decide to change trajectories, nobody says they quit. They say they switched careers. And if you find that this career isn't for you, you are fully within your rights to switch careers guilt-free.

Despite my feelings of being stuck from time to time, at the end of the day I still loved to write. And it was important for me to recognize that. It was crucial to ask myself "Do I love writing enough to put up with all the rest of the nonsense?" For me, so far, the answer has been yes.

So, instead of changing industries, I switched things up *within* the industry. My career has followed an unusual trajectory, bouncing from network multi-cam comedy to streaming drama to single-cam comedy. I never got showcased to the industry with meetings all over town, which happens to certain writers and actors. I was never in with the "in crowd." I scraped and clawed my way through and ended up figuring out a path that was never laid out for me.

In fact, it was only when I decided to forgo the approved pathways and do my own thing that I started to make serious progress. Sticking to what I thought I knew about how to make it in the industry was holding me back. Strictly abiding by what others had done before me was keeping me closed off to new possibilities and new ways to further my career.

That's why in the last section of this book, I want you to know that everything you have read up until now is the groundwork for you to build on. It should be used as a base. If in this book you see a certain path you want to take, by all means, go for it. But what will be more helpful is understanding the industry as it exists today, getting a feel for where it is going, and using all that knowledge to piece together your unique journey to get to the place you want to be.

Then you get to be the new voice driving this industry forward. You get to create storylines and characters nobody's ever seen before. You get to show us all how amazing TV really can be. And you get to show the business of TV what an amazing, creative, supportive, and inclusive workplace really is. You get to be the one who makes all aspects of TV better than they've ever been.

And while you're on your way, don't forget to look out for other things you like and/or want to do. It's great to have a goal or destination, but staying so singularly focused can leave you blind to possibilities that you might enjoy more than your current pursuit.

For better and for worse, entertainment is a wild industry. Don't forget to take the ups and downs with a grain of salt. Celebrate the good, don't fret too much over the bad, and always try to enjoy the thrilling, boring, hilarious, dramatic, important, and silly parts of this ridiculous career.

ACKNOWLEDGMENTS

I'd like to thank my family:

My mom, who has been a source for not just creative guidance, but the kind of unconditional motivation and support most people only read about in books.

My dad, for supporting me and introducing me to the music and comedy I would come to be inspired by for years to come.

My sister, Alexis, for being my writing whisperer and evergreen dream encourager.

My brother, Damien, whose love, friendship, and brotherhood showed me that family isn't just about who you grow up with.

My brother, John, who is the only thing still keeping this family on an even keel.

My niece and nephew, Ruby and Dominic, who already got the best shoutout in the book.

Mark, my TV writing partner, without whom I would have given up on this TV thing a long time ago.

My agent, Linda Konner, for being the no-nonsense New Yorker I needed to get this book out there.

Laurie Scheer, whose mentorship and advice helped me take an idea and make it into a sale-worthy book proposal.

And to those who made this book possible by literally being in the book: Lawrence Konner, Bob Daily, David Kohan, Robert Thompson, Michael Price, Evan Smith, Aaron W. Sala, Howard Jordan Jr., Michael Jamin, Heather Dean, and Sebastian Martínez-Kadlecik—this book would not have been the same without your perspectives and thoughtfulness.

GLOSSARY

A-Story / B-Story / C-Runner: The A-story is the main storyline in any given episode, usually involving the main character of the show. The B storyline is the second most important story and is given less screen time. C storylines follow in this same pattern but are sometimes so minor that in comedies they're downgraded to a "runner," meaning a repeated joke with no story arc.

Blocking: A directing term referring to the moves the actors will make during their scenes. Since the cameras and the sound and the viability of the scene depend on everyone being coordinated, the blocking is important to establish who's walking where, who comes into the scene when, and generally what the scene will look like on set.

Blow: Comedy-speak for the final joke in a scene. In traditional network sitcoms, you're expected to have a joke to end every single scene.

Blue Sky: The brainstorming period that takes place during the initial stages of a writers' room. This is the time when almost anything can be proposed.

Box Rental: The money paid by a studio or production company to rent supplies from the employee. For example, if you use your own laptop for work, you are owed a box rental.

Broadcast TV Season: Traditionally, the pilot season would happen in early spring. In May, the network "upfronts" would take place, in which the new fall TV shows were unveiled to advertisers. This is when you found out which pilots were picked up and which ones died a horrible death. Networks would then give TV shows that made the cut a thirteen-episode order. They would start the writers' room in the summer, and they would wrap up by the winter holidays. And all this time, productions are waiting to hear if they've gotten their "back nine," which is the continuation of the season, making for a full twenty-two episodes. If they don't get the "back nine," cancellation is imminent. A version of this system is still in place to a much more limited extent with broadcast networks.

Comedy TV Shows:

Multi-Cam Comedies: Four cameras shoot a scene simultaneously in a set. There is a studio audience, and the whole production feels like a play.

Single-Cam Comedies: Filmed like a movie, one shot at a time, this is what most comedy is today—*Barry, The Office, Atlanta.* (Hint: when you don't hear laughter, it's single-cam.)

Crafty: Short for "craft services." These are the snacks and meals that are put out on stages or sets that is free for all.

Deadline: Deadline.com is one of the most popular entertainment industry news outlets, along with The Hollywood Reporter and Variety.

Final Draft: This is *the* screenwriting software used in TV. Across the many TV shows I've worked on, this is the only software that's ever been used.

Flip the Dolphin: Changing the order of two words or sentences. Used primarily in comedy writers' rooms, this term began as a joke in an attempt to get an unwitting writer to use the invented term correctly without ever teaching it to them.

Freelance Script: An episode of a TV show written by someone outside of the regular writing staff.

Greenlight: When a network greenlights a TV show, they have decided to move forward and produce the show.

IATSE Local 871: The union that you must join if you take a job as a writers' assistant or script coordinator.

Intellectual Property: Otherwise known as IP, Intellectual Property is any book, comic, podcast, news article, toy, or other property around which a TV show or movie is developed. Marvel is the most famous example of an IP mill becoming its own studio.

Jump the Shark: In season 5, episode 3 of *Happy Days*, Fonzi water-skis over a shark. It was a crazy, hijinks-laden episode that deviated completely from where the series had begun. The term "jump the shark" is now used to describe when a TV show has gone too far and is no longer what it used to be.

Lock-Up: A set duty usually given to production assistants in which you stand at a corner or by a door and make sure nobody crosses into frame while the director is shooting.

Mini-Room: A small group of usually upper-level writers assembled to work on a TV show. Streamers and networks will bring together a mini-room to write multiple episodes, or sometimes an entire season of a show, often before greenlighting the series.

Nakamura: A joke or story point that fails in the beginning of the episode, causing all further references to it to die along with it.

Nielsen Ratings: A system by which special cable boxes that track viewership are given out all over the country. An approximate number of viewers is then extracted to give an average rating for each show on TV. They now have a slightly different system for tracking streaming.

Off on Script: A writer has been sent away from the writers' room by the showrunner to work on writing their episode.

On Demand:

AVOD: Advertising-based Video on Demand—A streaming service in which the content is free but ad-supported: traditionally YouTube, Tubi, and Roku, but now most streamers are including an AVOD subscription tier in their price plans.

SVOD: Subscription Video on Demand—Streaming that you pay for monthly: Netflix, Prime, Max, etc.

OWA: Open writing assignment—production companies and studios have a piece of intellectual property or a specific story they want to develop, and writers are brought in to pitch their take on the story. The studio/production company will choose which version they like the best and will then pay that writer to develop/write it. This process is called a "bake-off."

Overall Deals: Contracts that studios and networks sign with writers they want to work with in developing TV shows. Writers are generally paid a large salary to create shows for the studio and to simultaneously work in a writers' room for one of the studio's shows.

Packaging: The act of putting together a show—combining all the elements (actor, writer, producer, director). The fight against agency packaging is why every writer fired their agent in 2019.

Punch-Up: In comedy, when a script needs a pass (a rewrite of the script) to add jokes and make it funnier.

Residuals: Money given to writers after their initial script payment. Residuals can come from reruns, sales of international rights, streaming, episode purchases, recurring character payments, etc.

The Sony hacks: In 2014, Sony's servers were hacked by a North Korean group as retribution for daring to release the Seth Rogen movie *The Interview* about Kim Jong Un. A ton of embarrassing company emails and information were released to the public.

Specs:

Feature Spec: A wholly original feature film script that the writer has written on speculation, in the hopes that somebody will buy it. In this case, it means that nobody has commissioned them and they write it in the hopes of selling it afterwards.

TV Spec: An episode written of a TV show that is currently on the air. Up until the late 2000s, this was how writers got jobs working on TV shows. They would write a spec of *Friends* or *The Sopranos*, for example, and that script would be submitted by their agent for potential staffing.

Stunt Script: A screenplay written with the purpose of garnering attention rather than with the intention of getting it made.

Sweetening: The act of adjusting the laughter in a studio audience in post-production to make a laugh bigger than it really was.

WGA: The screenwriter's union—the Writers Guild of America.

Zoom Room: A virtual writers' room that meets on Zoom.

RESOURCES

ENTERTAINMENT JOB SITES

- Mandy.com
- EntertainmentCareers.net
- StaffMeUp.com
- Showbizjobs.com

FACEBOOK GROUPS

The "I need a . . ." Groups: Groups like "I need a production assistant" or "I need a production crew" are good places to start a job hunt. These groups are dedicated to staffing needs. Most of these groups are closed, but you can ask anyone you know who qualifies to check the groups for you until you qualify for entry.

The "Awesome Assistants" Groups: Not primarily focused on job hunting, these are still great resources for information and the occasional job posting. These groups are also closed.

PRODUCTION WEEKLY

Productionweekly.com: A weekly listing of all TV and film productions currently in operation, which charges a subscription for access. It gives you a list of detailed information for every production shooting right now, and often has phone numbers for their production offices.

REDDIT

Screenwriting Reddit: reddit.com/r/Screenwriting—an amazing resource and entire community where you can research competitions, fellowships, and workshops, and learn about screenwriting craft.

THE UTA JOB LIST/ANONYMOUS PRODUCTION ASSISTANT

The UTA Job List: Every couple of weeks, the United Talent Agency compiles a job list that circulates throughout the industry. Jobs on this list range from personal to executive assistant jobs, production assistant jobs, development, agency, and management company positions. And it can be found at the following site . . .

The Anonymous Production Assistant: For years, this website has provided information about being a production assistant and is one of the few places to consistently find the UTA Job List in addition to jobs they post separately from the list. (anonymousproductionassistant.com/uta-joblist)

SCREENWRITING COMPETITIONS

Academy Nicholl Fellowship: This is the Academy's screenwriting competition, as in the same people who do the Oscars. This is as big as it gets when it comes to competitions. Unfortunately, this is exclusively for feature scripts. There is no TV category.

Austin Film Festival Competitions: Held in nearly as high a regard as the Nicholl Fellowship, they accept features and TV pilots.

Slamdance Screenplay Competition: Though held in slightly lower esteem than The Nicholl Fellowship and the Austin Film Festival, people have good things to say about Slamdance, which has been around since 1995. Even if the name recognition isn't quite up to the levels of the previous two, contestants have applauded the prizes and the thorough feedback that entrants receive.

Tracking Board Launch Pad: A well-established competition with huge numbers of connections offered to winners. They feature a popular TV pilot competition.

PAGE International: Originally designed as a way to bridge the gap between reps and producers in LA and screenwriters outside of LA, the PAGE International Screenwriting competition has grown in popularity since it began in 2004. They have a long list of success stories and a deep trove of industry producers and executives who they've connected with past winners.

WORKSHOPS, FELLOWSHIPS, AND LABS

Warner Bros. Discovery Access Writers Program: A new name for a program with a long history. As of 2023, the WB TV Writers Workshop, which began over forty years ago and was one of the original studio writers' workshops, is now the WB Discovery Access Writers Program. In order to apply, you need two original pilots, two personal statements, a bio, résumé, and an intro video. If you're selected, participants will work on writing a new TV pilot and will learn about the business and writers' rooms from executives, writers, and producers. The program is one of many within WB Discovery Access, an entire department dedicated to elevating underrepresented voices. It's worth checking to see if any other programs might suit your career goals.

NBC Universal Launch: Formerly known as NBC's Writers on the Verge, the program has rebranded and focuses on supporting diverse writers. Similar to the WB program, participants receive mentorship from executives at NBC in addition to weekly workshops that help participants refine their work and/or write original pilots. This provides the same type of pipeline as WB, wherein, at the end of the program, the writers are put up for staffing opportunities at NBC Universal Studio's shows. NBC requires two original pilots in addition to a résumé and a personal essay to apply.

NBC Universal GTDI (Global Talent Development & Inclusion): This department contains three diversity programs, two of which are focused on feature screenwriting. However, the Universal Animation Writers Program includes both TV and film writers, focused on programming for ages 3-11. Applying requires an adapted script and one of either an original feature treatment, an original screenplay, a comedy packet, or an original pilot script. In addition, you'll need to submit a résumé and personal essay. This is a one-year full-time program in which participants will be paid a salary for the year. The program intends to develop your project to potentially get it on the air, but there are potential staffing opportunities available on NBC Universal programs at the end of the program.

Sesame Workshop Writers' Room: Run by Sesame Street, the Sesame Workshop is a diversity initiative focused on children's television. Eight applicants are selected, and the program involves mentorship from industry professionals as well as a workshop to create a children's TV pilot. At the end of the workshop, two participants are picked to further develop their ideas. To apply, you'll need a children's television sample (which is generally a short eleven-page script), a résumé, and a personal statement.

Nickelodeon Writing Program: This is a seriously robust workshop. It's a year-long, full-time, paid opportunity. Like the Sesame Workshop, it is focused on creating kids' TV. However, Nickelodeon is geared toward a wider range of ages. In your application they'll ask you to specify whether you're interested in writing Preschool Content (ages 2 to 6), Kids' Content (ages 6 to 11), or Preteen/Young Adult Content (ages 11 to 17). You'll need a spec script, an original pilot script, and a résumé to apply.

Fox Entertainment Writers Incubator: Very similar to the WB and NBC programs, the Fox Entertainment Writers Incubator is a three-month program in which four diverse applicants are selected to work on their samples and meet and learn from industry professionals. At the conclusion of the workshop, Fox promises priority in staffing meetings on the studio's shows. Though they only require one original TV pilot script to enter, they do have a fairly long list of other requirements, including a personal statement, résumé, bio, script synopsis, two additional loglines for different TV show ideas, and two references.

Disney Entertainment Television Writing Program: This program has been around for over thirty years and is similar to the Nickelodeon program in that participants become full-time employees of Disney for one year and are given a salary. They offer mentorship and access to a slew of working professionals and writing program alumni, which includes some real heavy hitters. You will need two original pilots, a personal essay, a résumé, and a "pitch" detailing why you should be considered.

Paramount Writers Mentoring Program: A sixteen-week program in which you meet with studio executives and mentors to help you prepare for a career in TV and to work on your samples. This program is more akin to WB and NBC, rather than the Nickelodeon and Disney full-time paid models. To apply, Paramount requires one original pilot and one spec script, a résumé, and a personal essay.

Sundance Institute Episodic Lab: A six-day program in Utah in which participants' TV scripts are workshopped with mentors, showrunners, and executives in a simulated writers' room. Though not connected to a major studio, Sundance is such a huge name in the industry that being a program alum could mean major connections and networking opportunities moving forward. The application is quite extensive and includes an original TV pilot, a synopsis, a series overview, a personal statement, a thematic statement, answering a set of creative questions about your project, and a bio.

Humanitas New Voices Fellowship: Founded in 2010, this program is focused on finding unrepresented voices in TV and film and creating mentorship and networking opportunities.

The Black List x WIF Episodic Lab: The Black List has become an important name in the industry, putting out a list every year of the most talked-about scripts within the industry. This has helped elevate many screenwriters and has led to the sale of several feature scripts. On the TV side, The Black List has partnered with WIF (Women In Film) for the Black List x WIF Episodic Lab, a four-week program for female TV screenwriters to learn from mentors and to hone their scripts.

INDEX

ABOUT THE AUTHOR

ANTON SCHETTINI is a screenwriter, producer, and author. He has worked in fourteen different TV writers' rooms, which has included writing scripts for prime time TV comedies on CBS and writing/producing a series on AMC Networks. A native New Yorker, Anton betrayed his East Coast roots and moved to Los Angeles to pursue screenwriting, slowly and steadily rising up in the industry. This provided him with a deep knowledge of the various paths, obstacles, drudgery, and opportunity that together make up a TV writing career. He hopes to share this knowledge with the next wave of TV writers.